W9-DHR-855

Budapest

POLAND

CZECHOSLOVAKIA

U.S.S.R

AUSTRIA

Budapest

HUNGARY

ROMANIA

YUGOSLAVIA

Adriatic Sea

ITALY

HarperCollins*Publishers*

This book was produced using QuarkXPress™ and
Adobe Illustrator 88™ on Apple Macintosh™ computers
and output to separated film on a Linotronic™ 300 Imagesetter

Photography: Tim Sharman
Cartography: Susan Harvey Design
Design: Kerry Aylin

First published 1991
Copyright © HarperCollins Publishers
Printed and published by HarperCollins Publishers
ISBN 0 00 435755-8

HOW TO USE THIS BOOK

Your Collins Traveller Guide will help you find your way around your holiday destination quickly and easily. It is split into two sections which are colour-coded:

The blue section provides you with an alphabetical sequence of headings, from **ART GALLERIES** to **WALKS** via **EXCURSIONS**, **RESTAURANTS**, **SHOPPING** etc. Each entry within a topic includes information on how to get there, how much it will cost you, when it will be open and what to expect. Furthermore, every page has its own map showing the position of each item and the nearest landmark. This allows you to orientate yourself quickly and easily in your new surroundings.

To find what you want to do - having dinner, visiting a museum, going for a walk or shopping for gifts - simply flick through the blue headings and take your pick!

The red section is an alphabetical list of information. It provides essential facts about places and cultural items – 'What is the Országház?', 'Who was Saint Stephen?', 'Where is Visegrád?' – and expands on subjects touched on in the first half of the book. This section also contains practical travel information. It ranges through how to find accommodation, where to hire a car, the variety of eating places and food available, tips on health, information on money, which newspapers are available, how to find a taxi and where the Youth Hostels are. It is lively and informative and easy to use. Each band shows the first three letters of the first entry on the page. Simply flick through the bands till you find the entry you need!

All the main entries are also cross-referenced to help you find them. Names in small capitals – **CHILDREN** – tell you that there is more information about the item you are looking for under the topic on churches in the first part of the book. So when you read 'see **CHILDREN**' you turn to the blue heading for **CHILDREN**. The instruction 'see **A-Z**', after a word, lets you know that the word has its own entry in the second part of the book. Similarly words in bold type – **Duna** – also let you know that there is an entry in the gazetteer for the indicated name. In both cases you just look under the appropriate heading in the red section. Packed full of information and easy to use - you'll always know where you are with your Collins Traveller Guide!

ORSZÁGHÁZ

Kossuth
Lajos
tér

Alkotmány u.

Hold utca

Báthori utca

Széchenyi Rakpart

Münnich Ferenc u.

Szabadság tér

Alpári Gyula u.

MAGYAR
TUDOMÁNYOS
AKADÉMIA

Roosevelt tér

Zrínyi u.

GRESHAM
PALOTA

Széchenyi
lánchíd

József Attila u.

Bécsi u.

Nádor u.

József n.

FORUM

Vörösmarty
tér

Deák

Petőfi

Ferenc

Vigadó u.

Váci utca

Csere J. u.

Belgrád

Danube

Szab

Erzsébet Híd

INTRODUCTION

Hungary is one of the easiest and most attractive Eastern-European countries to visit, and its capital, Budapest, is a lively metropolis of over 2.3 million people, the product of the union in 1872 between three historically separate communities, Óbuda (old Buda) and Buda on the western bank of the Danube, and Pest on the eastern bank. Politically and commercially it is one of the most important cities in Eastern Europe, but Budapest is also a focal point of culture and a city of great beauty, the 'Pearl of the Danube', an historic and romantic spot which attracts millions of visitors every year. The Hungarian people are descended from Magyar nomads from central Asia who settled on the banks of the Danube at the end of the 9thC. The Magyars conquered the existing miscellaneous tribes who had occupied the area since the 4thC when the Roman Empire had begun to shrivel and collapse. The Danube once formed the northern border (*limes*) of the empire, and the Roman military settlement of Aquincum, now the district of Óbuda, had been the flourishing capital of the Roman Province of Lower Pannonia. A century after the Magyars settled, the state of Hungary was officially established, and crowned its first king Stephen (István) I (997-1038), according to legend, on Christmas Day 1000. He began the conversion of the pagan Magyars to Christianity and reorganized the administrative divisions of the country along the lines of other European feudal states. Buda became established as the seat of Hungarian royalty and the main population centre, while Pest gradually evolved as a smaller commercial and trading centre at the important river crossing, populated mainly by craftsmen and merchants. During the passage of centuries these twin settlements astride the Danube endured a turbulent and tragic litany of wars, invasions, occupations and oppression. In 1241 both communities narrowly escaped complete annihilation during the Mongol invasions, which prompted the erection of the first Castle and Royal Palace on Buda hill by King Béla IV. The Turks invaded in 1541 and remained in occupation until the reconquest in 1686 by the Hapsburg armies of Charles of Lorraine. In 1848 Budapest witnessed the outbreak of the Hungarian Revolution, during which the poet Sándor Petőfi was killed, and many others lost their lives in the brutal suppression which followed the challenge to Hapsburg absolutism. In the 20thC, the city suffered severely

during World War II, when almost 70% of Budapest's buildings were damaged and all the Danube bridges blown up. Post-war Soviet control of Hungary was challenged in the popular uprising of 1956, when over 3000 lost their lives and 200,000 fled the country as the tanks moved into the city to crush the opposition. In the years following the uprising, Hungary's communist leaders recognized the need for certain measures of economic and political liberalization ('market socialism'), with the result that Hungary has escaped the terminal stagnation prevalent in other countries of Eastern Europe now emerging into economic and political freedom after decades of Soviet domination, and is an attractive holiday destination which places no restrictions on tourists.

And as a tourist attraction Budapest has plenty to offer. Historic sites, museums and galleries, Turkish baths, cheap night-time entertainment (including a casino), plentiful and reasonably-priced restaurants, relaxing cafés and coffee-houses, a cheap and efficient transport system, and, of course, a friendly and welcoming citizenry.

Buda on the hilly west bank is famous for its Castle District, a long, narrow plateau filled with medieval streets, courtyards and architectural monuments. You can reach the area on foot from the river, or take the *sikló*, a miniature railway which runs from Clark Ádám tér at the western end of Chain Bridge (Széchenyi lánchíd) to Buda Palace. Trinity Square contains one of the most notable sights, Matthias Church,

originally dating from the 13thC, but extended in the 15thC by King Matthias. In 1541 the Turks converted the building into a mosque; it was later extended and baroquized after the reconquest, and its present neo-Gothic form dates from renovation in the 1800s. From the Fisherman's Bastion the panorama of the city, straddling the Danube with its bridges, is spectacular, especially at night when you can admire the imposing floodlit facade of the Gothic-style Parliament with its impressive dome, which dominates the Pest bank of the river. The towers and colonnades of the Bastion and the decorative tiling of Matthias Church are reflected in the copper-glass facade of the nearby Hilton Hotel, whose modern design ingeniously incorporates sections of a 13thC Dominican Monastery. Away from the crowds in Trinity Square, the medieval streets of the district are easily explored on foot. Among the many points of interest are the reconstructed Vienna Gate (Bécsi kapu) which marks the northern entrance to the district, Fortuna utca with its fine baroque buildings and Úri utca from where you can enter the caves and passageways under the hill, used as shelters during a succession of conflicts from the Middle Ages to World War II. In Trinity Street you will find the famous Ruszwurm Café, the oldest in Budapest (1827), only one of many cafés and restaurants in which to take refreshment before exploring the Royal Palace with its historic buildings, Historical Museum, National Gallery and Széchenyi National Library.

Outside the Castle District itself, Gellért Hill to the south provides another excellent panorama of the city. At the top of this steep limestone escarpment is the Liberation Monument erected in 1947 to commemorate Hungary's liberation in World War II, and behind it is the Citadel built by the Austrians in the mid-19thC, from where a spectacular fireworks display is mounted annually on St. Stephen's Day, 20 August. Nearby are the Gellért Baths, the most famous bathing complex in a country which from Roman times has been renowned for its hot mineral springs. Valued for their cleansing and medicinal benefits, they are also popular meeting places, and the city has five traditional copper-domed Turkish baths in addition to the Gellért Hotel facilities. If the budget can't stretch to a dip in the Gellért establishment, there are more reasonable rates at the Rudas Baths at the foot of the hill near the Erzsébet Bridge. These baths, built by Pasha Mustapha in 1566, are for men only, but further north on the same side of the river are the Király Baths, a rambling edifice of traditional Turkish design with baroque and neoclassical additions, which are open to both sexes on different days. Another reminder of the Turkish occupation of the city can be found in Rózsadomb (Rose Hill), an up-market residential district north of the Castle District, where you can find the Tomb of Gül Baba ('Father of the Roses') a 16thC Muslim shrine to a dervish who died in the presence of the Pasha of Buda during a service in Matthias Church (then a mosque).
Further north in Óbuda are the remains of prehistoric, Roman and early Christian settlements,

of which the most interesting are the remains of the Roman town of Aquincum, once a flourishing frontier outpost of 6000 soldiers which also supported a civilian population of 30,000. The Buda Hills, to the northwest, are a popular recreation spot and ideal for family trips. This scenic area can be visited on the cog-wheel railway from Városmajor Park, and the hills can be explored using the Pioneer Railway which is staffed by children, and by the Jánoshegy chairlift.

In contrast to the historic and scenic attractions of Buda and Óbuda, Pest on the eastern bank of the Danube is a graceful, mainly 19thC section whose fine boulevards, public and commercial buildings, elegant shops, restaurants and pavement cafés, prompt comparison with Paris. In Belváros (Inner Town), little of the old medieval Pest has survived the extensive 19thC building programme. Váci utca, the main shopping street, is filled with boutiques, selling both Hungarian and international fashions, hotels, and smart modern commercial offices. It leads into

Vörösmarty tér, Pest's elegant central square, where tourists and street artists congregate around the statue of one of Hungary's most famous poets, Mihaly Vörösmarty (1800-50). Nearby is Roosevelt tér, site of the Hungarian Academy of Sciences and the Art Nouveau Gresham Palace. From here you can promenade along the Danube past the Romantic-style Vigadó Cultural Centre, and enjoy the views of Buda on the opposite bank. Another major attraction is Városliget, the city's largest park, reached from the centre via Andrássy út,

Budapest's grandest boulevard which is lined with many graceful buildings. The park has a plethora of recreational and cultural facilities including a zoo, circus, museums, the Széchenyi baths, a funfair and sports halls. You may also like to visit Budapest's other main leisure centre, Margaret Island (named after the daughter of King Béla IV), across the Árpád Bridge. This is a traffic-free oasis of parkland and gardens, with thermal baths, fountains, sculptures, a water tower and ecclesiastical ruins.

Finally, if you tire of the city and the immediate locality, then just 20 km to the north is the beautiful Danube Bend region, graced by the historic, romantic and picturesque towns of Szentendre, Esztergom (the ancient residence of Hungarian royalty), Vác and Visegrád, set in spectacular scenery – the 'Hungarian Wachau' – and ideal for a one- or two-day trip from the capital. Unquestionably, if you are planning to explore the newly-accessible countries and capitals of Eastern Europe, and have not yet visited Budapest, then this wonderful city should head your itinerary.

EMKE HBH

Erzsébet krt.

Teréz krt.

TROJKA

TOKAJI

Andrássy út

GÖSSER

Váci u.

Kossuth
Lajos
tér

GRESHAM

Roosevelt tér

D a n u b e

WERNERSGRÜNER FREGATT

GELLÉRTHEGY

Szarvas
tér

SZARVAS
PINCE

V á r h e g y

ARANYFÁCÁN

ARANYFÁCÁN II, Szilágyi Erzsébet fasor 33.
❑ 1200-2400. Bus 5, 22, 56, 156; Tram 18, 56; M Moszkva tér.
This bar/restaurant serves Czechoslovakian beer and Hungarian food.

EMKE HBH VII, Akácfa u. 1-3.
❑ 1100-2400. Bus 7, 7A, 78; M Blaha Lujza tér.
*One of the HBH chain, serving excellent beer brewed on the premises
and very good food (though the menu is limited).*

FREGATT V, Molnár u. 26.
❑ 1500-2300 Mon.-Sat., 1700-2400 Sun. Bus 15; Tram 2, 2A.
The closest thing in Budapest to an English pub (with dartboard!).

GÖSSER V, Régipósta u. 4.
❑ 1000-2200 Mon.-Sat., 1500-2200 Sun. M Vörösmarty tér.
Imported Austrian draught beer and sandwiches. Can be very busy.

GRESHAM Gresham-palota: V, Roosevelt tér 5.
❑ 1200-2300. Bus 2, 4, 16; Tram 2.
Situated in a stunning building, and offering a varied selection of wines.

SZARVAS PINCE I, Szarvas tér 2.
❑ 1200-0100. Bus 5, 78, 86; Tram 18, 49.
Pricey wine cellar, popular with tourists. Food in adjoining restaurant.

TOKAJI VI, Andrássy út 20.
❑ 1200-2300. Bus 1, 4, 4A; M Opera.
Specializes in Tokaji *wines – the szamorodni is excellent (see* **Drinks***).*

TROJKA VI, Andrássy út 28.
❑ 1100-0600. Bus 1, 4, 4A; M Opera.
Good selection of wines and beers, and excellent and imaginative food.

WERNERSGRÜNER V, Váci u. 61.
❑ 0800-2400. M Felszabadulás tér.
East German beers. Advisable to go early if you want a seat.

VÁROSLIGET

VAJDAHUNYAD VÁRA

FŐVÁROSI TANÁCS

Városház u.

Erzsébet krt.

Andrássy út

OPERAHÁZ

Teréz krt.

NYUGATI PÁLYAUDVAR

Kossuth Lajos tér

ORSZÁGHÁZ

Danube

BUDAPEST HILTON

Várhegy

KIRÁLYI PALOTA

CITADELLA

GELLÉRTHEGY

KIRÁLYI PALOTA (ROYAL PALACE) I, Várhegy.
Bus 16, 16A; Funicular railway from Clark Ádám tér.
An impressive cluster of buildings on the site of King Béla IV's 13thC palace. It houses two major museums. See MUSEUMS 1, WALK 2, **A-Z**.

ORSZÁGHÁZ (PARLIAMENT) V, Kossuth Lajos tér 1-3.
Bus 15; Tram 2, 2A; Trolleybus 70, 78; M Kossuth tér.
A neo-Gothic building, reminiscent of Westminster and with a richly-decorated interior. Guided tours are available. See WALK 1, **A-Z**.

OPERAHÁZ (OPERA HOUSE) VI, Andrássy út 22.
❑ Times of visits marked up on board outside. Bus 1, 4, 4A; M Opera.
A late-19thC neo-Renaissance building. See CULTURE, WALK 3, **A-Z**.

CITADELLA I, Gellérthegy 33.
Bus 27. ❑ 10 Ft.
A mid-19thC fortress crowning Gellért Hill (see PARKS, **Gellérthegy**) *and today housing a café, hotel, and restaurant. See* **A-Z**.

BUDAPEST HILTON I, Hess András tér 1-3.
Bus 16, 16A.
An architecturally controversial modern building which incorporates the ruins of a Dominican church and a Jesuit monastery. See WALK 2, **A-Z**.

FŐVÁROSI TANÁCS (CITY HALL) V, Városház u. 9-11.
Bus 1, 9; M Deák Ferenc tér.
The largest baroque building in Budapest. See **A-Z**.

NYUGATI PÁLYAUDVAR (WESTERN RAILWAY STATION)
VI, Teréz krt. 109. M Nyugati pályaudvar.
Built by the Eiffel Company to Victor Bernhardt and Auguste de Serres's design. Restoration work highlights the glass and cast-iron frontage.

VAJDAHUNYAD VÁRA Városliget: XIV.
❑ 1000-1800 Tue.-Sun. Bus 1, 4, 4A; Trolleybus 72, 75; M Hősök tere.
This castle is an eccentric amalgamation of architectural styles. See **A-Z**.

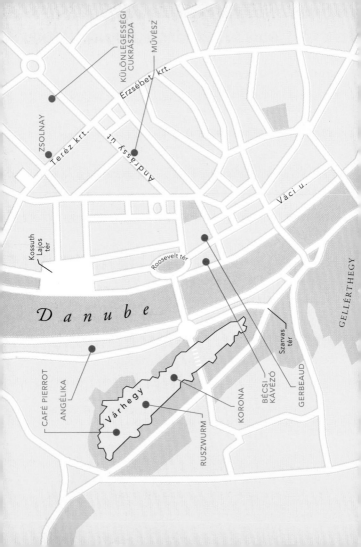

KÜLÖNLEGESSÉGI
CUKRÁSZDA

MŰVÉSZ

Erzsébet krt.

ZSOLNAY

Teréz krt.

Andrássy út

Váci u.

Kossuth
Lajos
tér

Roosevelt tér

D a n u b e

GELLÉRTHEGY

CAFÉ PIERROT

ANGÉLIKA

Várhegy

RUSZWURM

KORONA

BÉCSI
KÁVÉZÓ

GERBEAUD

Szarvas
tér

ANGÉLIKA I, Batthyány tér 7.
❑ 1200-2000 Mon. & Fri., 1000-2000 Tue.-Thu., Sat., Sun. Bus 11, 39.
Old-style café next to Szent Anna-templom (see **CHURCHES**, **A-Z**), *in a building which was formerly the vicarage. Frequented mostly by locals.*

BÉCSI KÁVÉZÓ Forum Hotel: V, Apáczai Csere János u. 12-14.
❑ 1900-2100. Bus 2; Tram 2, 2A; M Vörösmarty tér.
The cakes are mouthwatering and the vanilla sauce even more so.

GERBEAUD V, Vörösmarty tér 7.
❑ 0900-2100. Bus 2, 15; M Vörösmarty tér.
Everybody's favourite, so the service may be a bit slow! See **WALK 1**.

KORONA I, Dísz tér 16.
❑ 1000-2100. Bus 16, 16A; Funicular railway from Clark Ádám tér.
A tempting array of cakes. Poetry readings some evenings. See **WALK 2**.

KÜLÖNLEGESSÉGI CUKRÁSZDA VI, Andrássy út 70.
❑ 0900-2000. Bus 1, 4, 4A; M Vörösmarty utca.
Formerly owned by a renowned pastry chef and spectacularly decorated.

MŰVÉSZ VI, Andrássy út 29.
❑ 0800-2000. Bus 1, 4, 4A; M Opera.
Owing to its position, this café is frequented by theatre staff.

CAFÉ PIERROT I, Fortuna u. 14.
❑ 1700-0100 Mon.-Sat., 1000-2300 Sun. Bus 16, 16A.
Oriental decor and background music provided by a piano player.

RUSZWURM I, Szentháromság tér 7.
❑ 1000-2000 Thu.-Tue. Bus 16, 16A.
A wide variety of delicious cakes which are baked on the premises.

ZSOLNAY Béke Radisson Hotel: VI, Teréz krt. 97.
❑ 0900-2000. Bus 12, 12A; Tram 4, 6.
The cakes here are served on hand-painted Zsolnay porcelain.

NÉPLIGET

PLANETÁRIUM

VIDÁM PARK

FŐVÁROSI NAGYCIRKUSZ

VÁROSLIGET

Állatkerti krt.

Városház u.

FŐVÁROSI ÁLLAT ÉS NÖVÉNYKERT

Erzsébet krt.

Andrássy út

Teréz krt.

Kossuth Lajos tér

Danube

GELLÉRTHEGY

Várhegy

VIASZMÚZEUM ÉS ALAGÚTRENDSZER

SKANZEN

ÚTTÖRŐVASÚT

FŐVÁROSI ÁLLAT ÉS NÖVÉNYKERT (BUDAPEST ZOO)
Városliget, Állatkerti krt. 6-12.
❏ 0900-1800 (summer), 0900-1600 (winter). Trolleybus 72. ❏ 5 Ft.
The home of over 3000 animals. Especially popular with the children are the animal nursery and the Oriental elephant house.

VIDÁM PARK (AMUSEMENT PARK)
Városliget, Állatkerti krt. 14-16.
❏ 1000-2000 (often closes in winter). Trolleybus 72; M Hősök tere.
Not the most up-to-date of amusement parks, but still great fun.

FŐVÁROSI NAGYCIRKUSZ (MUNICIPAL CIRCUS)
Városliget, Állatkerti krt. 7.
❏ 2000 Tue., Wed.; 1700, 2000 Thu., Fri.; 1000, 1700, 2000 Sat., Sun. Trolleybus 72; M Hősök tere.
Traditional circus performances are held in this modern (1971) building.

PLANETÁRIUM X, Népliget.
❏ Wed.-Mon. Bus 182; Trolleybus 75; M Népliget. ❏ 35 Ft.
A spectacular light and sound performance. The Studio's Laser Theatre situated here has one-hour shows on Mon. & Thu. 1800, 1930 (150 Ft).

VIASZMÚZEUM ÉS ALAGÚTRENDSZER I, Úri u. 9.
❏ Tue.-Sun. 1000-1800. Bus 16, 16A.
A waxwork display depicting scenes from Hungarian history in one of the Castle District caves.

ÚTTÖRŐVASÚT (PIONEER RAILWAY)
Budai-hegység: Széchenyi-hegy to Hűvösvölgy.
Bus 21, 90, 190; Tram 56; cog-wheel railway upper terminus.
A 12 km-long railway line run (but not driven) by children, taking you up to the vantage point of Jánoshegy in the Buda Hills (see PARKS).

SKANZEN (VILLAGE MUSEUM) Pilisszentlászló.
Genuine village houses and buildings taken from the surrounding countryside and reassembled to form an old-style village. See EXCURSION 1.

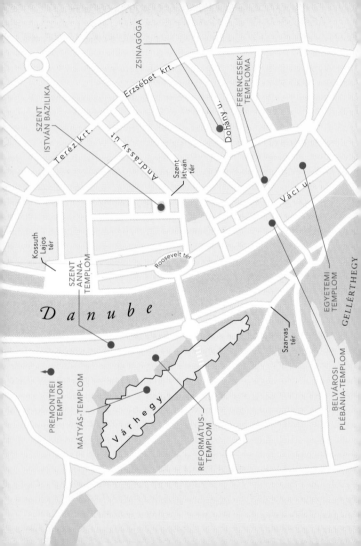

SZENT ISTVÁN BAZILIKA

ZSINAGÓGA

Erzsébet krt.

FERENCESEK TEMPLOMA

Dohány u.

Teréz krt.

Andrássy út

Szent István tér

Váci u.

Kossuth Lajos tér

SZENT ANNA-TEMPLOM

Roosevelt tér

EGYETEMI TEMPLOM

GELLÉRTHEGY

D a n u b e

Szarvas tér

BELVÁROSI PLÉBÁNIA-TEMPLOM

PREMONTREI TEMPLOM

MÁTYÁS-TEMPLOM

Várhegy

REFORMÁTUS-TEMPLOM

MÁTYÁS-TEMPLOM I, Szentháromság tér.
Bus 16, 16A.
Originally founded in the 13thC but named after King Matthias who undertook extensive reconstruction in the 15thC. See **WALK 2**, **A-Z**.

SZENT ISTVÁN BAZILIKA V, Szent István tér.
Bus 1, 4, 4A, 182; M Arany János u.
Largest church in the capital, neo-Renaissance in style. See **WALK 1**, **A-Z**.

BELVÁROSI PLÉBÁNIA-TEMPLOM V, Március 15 tér
Bus 5, 7, 7A, 8, 8A; Tram 2.
The Inner City Parish Church, the oldest building in Budapest. See **A-Z**.

PREMONTREI TEMPLOM Margitsziget.
Via Árpád híd or Margit híd; Bus 26.
The tower of this chapel houses the oldest bell in Hungary. See **A-Z**.

SZENT ANNA-TEMPLOM Batthyány tér.
Bus 11, 39, 60, 86; Tram 9. 19; M Batthyány tér.
Baroque church much influenced by Italian architectural styles. See **A-Z**.

REFORMÁTUS-TEMPLOM Szilágyi Dezső tér.
Bus 86; Tram 9, 19.
In a five-pointed star shape, symbolic of the Reformed Church. See **A-Z**.

ZSINAGÓGA VII, Dohány u. 2-8.
❑ 1000-1300 Mon.-Fri. Bus 1; Tram 47, 49; Trolleybus 74; M Astoria.
Byzantine-Moorish synagogue which is being restored. See **WALK 3**, **A-Z**.

EGYETEMI TEMPLOM V, Eötvös Loránd u. 7.
Bus 15; M Kálvin tér.
Built in 1725-42 for the monks of the Order of St. Paul. See **A-Z**.

FERENCESEK TEMPLOMA V, Felszabadulás tér.
Bus 5, 7, 7A, 8, 8A; M Felszabadulás tér.
Neo-Gothic church. Contains The Flood Mariner. See **WALK 1**, **A-Z**.

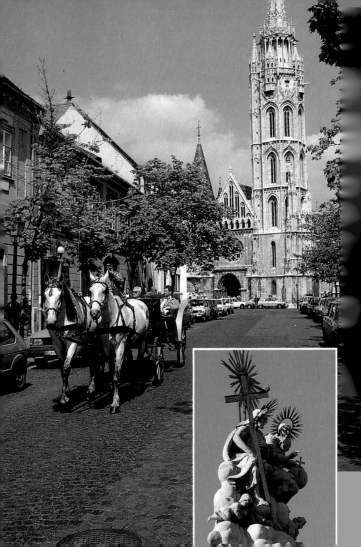

ASHÁZY

VÁROSLIGET

MILLENNIUMI
EMLÉKMŰ

Erzsébet krt.

Teréz krt.

Andrássy út

Városház u.

SZENT GELLÉRT EMLÉKMŰ

SZABADSÁG SZOBOR

HALÁSZBÁSTYA

Kossuth
Lajos
tér

ERZSÉBET
SZOBOR

GELLÉRTHEGY

Danube

Erzsébet híd

BÉCSI KAPU

Martirok útja

Várhegy

SZENT
ISTVÁN
SZOBOR

GÜL
BABA
TÜRBÉJE

MAGDOLNA
TORONY

SZABADSÁG SZOBOR (LIBERATION MONUMENT)

XI, beside the Citadella, Gellérthegy. Bus 27. ❑ 10 Ft.
*Commemorates the liberation of Hungary by the Soviet Army. See **A-Z**.*

SZENT ISTVÁN SZOBOR (ST. STEPHEN)

I, Szentháromság tér. Bus 16, 16A.
*A statue of the Hungarian King, Stephen I (see **István**), by Alajos Stróbl.*

MILLENNIUMI EMLÉKMŰ (MILLENNIUM MEMORIAL)

XIV, Hősök tere. Bus 1, 4, 4A, 20, 30; Trolleybus 75, 79; M Hősök tere.
*A 36 m-high column commemorating the thousandth anniversary, in 1897, of the conquest of the country. See **A-Z**.*

BÉCSI KAPU (VIENNA GATE) I, Bécsi kapu tér.

Bus 16, 16A.
*The northern entrance to the Castle District. Great views. See **WALK 2**.*

HALÁSZBÁSTYA (FISHERMEN'S BASTION) I, Castle Hill.

Bus 16, 16A.
*A cocktail of neo-Romanesque and neo-Gothic styles. See **WALK 2**, **A-Z**.*

GÜL BABA TÜRBÉJE (GÜL BABA'S TOMB) II, Mecset u. 14.

Bus 91, 191.
The carefully restored mausoleum of Gül Baba, a 16thC dervish.

MAGDOLNA TORONY I, Kapisztrán tér.

Bus 16, 16A.
*This tower is all that remains of a 13thC church. See **WALK 2**.*

ERZSÉBET SZOBOR (QUEEN ELIZABETH)

I, Buda end of Erzsébet híd. Bus 1, 5, 7, 7A, 8, 78, 112.
Statue representing the well-loved queen who was assassinated in 1898.

SZENT GELLÉRT EMLÉKMŰ XI, Gellérthegy.

Bus 27.
*An imposing monument overlooking the Danube. See **Gellért**.*

AQUINCUM

LAPIDARIUM

AMFITEÁTRUM

Szentendrei út

Danube

HERCULES
VILLA

DOMONKOS
KOLOSTOR

M A R G I T S Z I G E T

CONTRA
AQUINCUM

AQUINCUM III, Szentendrei út 139.
Bus 42, 143; Suburban railway (HÉV) from Batthyány tér.
Rich in archaeological treasures, this is the excavated site of the civic town of Aquincum which was founded by the Romans in the 1stC AD. See MUSEUMS 1, **A-Z**.

LAPIDARIUM III, Szentendrei út 139.
Bus 42, 143; Suburban railway (HÉV) from Batthyány tér.
Almost completely surrounds the Aquincum museum (see MUSEUMS 1*) and contains all kinds of stone carvings, reliefs, gravestones, sarcophagi and columns inscribed in Latin.*

AMFITEÁTRUM III, Szentendrei út.
Bus 42, 143; Suburban railway (HÉV) from Batthyány tér.
Dating from around AD 160, this site was unearthed in 1937-40 to reveal a large amphitheatre which could accommodate 7500 spectators. The arena measures 80 m by 90 m.

HERCULES VILLA III, Meggyfa u. 21.
Bus 18, 37, 42, 134, 137, 142.
A large Roman villa which contained some of the finest mosaic floors to be found in all Pannonia, depicting scenes from Hercules' life. Ruins can be seen around the modern school.

CONTRA AQUINCUM V, Március 15 tér.
Bus 5, 7, 7A, 8, 8A, 15, 78.
What is left of an old fortress, dating back to 292 BC, which was the first Roman settlement in Pest – at the time the western border of the Empire was the Danube.

DOMONKOS KOLOSTOR (DOMINICAN CONVENT)
Margitsziget.
Via Árpád híd or Margit híd; Bus 26.
Discovered in 1838 after the great flood, these ruins on Margaret Island (see PARKS, **Margitsziget***) are all that is left of the convent built by King Béla IV for his daughter Margaret.*

Hungária krt.

NÉPSTADION

BUDAPEST
SPORTCSARNOK

Köztársaság tér

VÁROSLIGET

LISZT FERENC
ZENEMŰVÉSZETI
FŐISKOLA

ERKEL SZÍNHÁZ

FŐVÁROSI
OPERETTSZÍNHÁZ

Liszt
Ferenc
tér

MADÁCH
SZÍNHÁZ

Erzsébet krt.

Teréz krt.

Andrássy út

VÍGSZÍNHÁZ

Szent István krt.

Kossuth
Lajos
tér

MAGYAR
ÁLLAMI
OPERAHÁZ

Belgrád

GELLÉRTHEGY

Danube

PESTI
VIGADÓ

DOMINICAN
COURT

Várhegy

CULTURE

MAGYAR ÁLLAMI OPERAHÁZ VI, Andrássy út 22.
❑ Operas 1900, concerts 1930. Bus 1, 4, 4A; M Opera.
A magnificent building which is the setting for the Hungarian state opera company. Formal dress is required. See BUILDINGS, WALK 3, **Operaház**.

ERKEL SZÍNHÁZ VIII, Köztársaság tér 30.
Bus 89, 99; Tram 28, 29, 37; M Keleti pályaudvar.
Large and spacious stage, particularly good for ballets and operas.

LISZT FERENC ZENEMŰVÉSZETI FŐISKOLA VI, Liszt tér 8.
Bus 1, 4, 4A, 12, 12A; Tram 4, 6; M November 7 tér.
This building functions as an academy and a concert hall. See WALK 3.

PESTI VIGADÓ V, Vigadó tér 1.
Bus 2, 15; Tram 2, 2A; M Vörösmarty tér.
Popular venue for concerts and recitals. Rich decor. See WALK 1.

DOMINICAN COURT Hilton Hotel: I, Hess András tér 1-3.
Bus 16, 16A.
An open-air venue which stages concerts and plays in the summertime.

FŐVÁROSI OPERETTSZÍNHÁZ VI, Nagymező u. 17.
❑ Performances at 1900. Tram 70, 78; M Opera.
Operettas by Imre Kálmán and Franz Lehár as well as popular musicals.

VÍGSZÍNHÁZ (COMEDY THEATRE) XIII, Szent István krt. 14.
Bus 12, 15, 33; Tram 4, 6; M Nyugati pályaudvar.
A large and varied repertoire of plays as well as the occasional musical.

MADÁCH SZÍNHÁZ (THEATRE) VII, Teréz krt. 29-33.
Bus 12, 12A; Tram 4, 6.
This company has successfully staged musicals for several years.

BUDAPEST SPORTCSARNOK XIV, Népstadion út 2.
Bus 55, 95; Tram 75; M Népstadion.
Venue for international indoor sports events, pop and rock concerts.

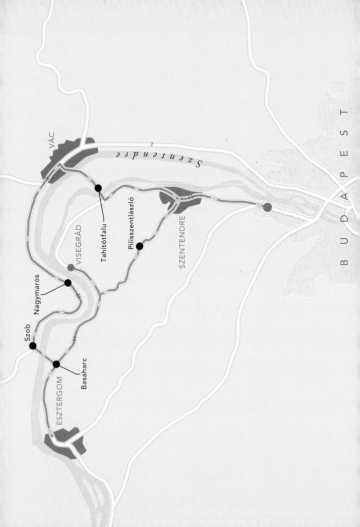

VÁC

Szentendre

BUDAPEST

VISEGRÁD

Tahitótfalu

Pilisszentlászló

SZENTENDRE

Nagymaros

Szob

ESZTERGOM

Basaharc

A one-day excursion exploring the towns on the banks of the Danube to the north of Budapest.

Take Road 11, heading north out of Budapest.

19 km – Szentendre (see **A-Z**). This beautiful little town is a favourite with artists. The central square, Fő tér, has a wrought-iron cross built by Serbian merchants in 1763 to commemorate the town's survival of a devastating plague. The narrow alley in the northwest corner of the square leads up to Várdomb (Castle Hill) which is a good place from which to survey the charms of this settlement with its winding streets and numerous churches. On the hill behind is the Catholic Parish

Szentendre

Church, the baroque additions mask most of its original medieval and Gothic features, though a sundial from the earlier period remains. Behind the church is the Czóbel Béla Múzeum which houses a collection of paintings by this artist. The orthodox episcopal Belgrade Church can be found in its own walled garden in Alkotmány utca. It was built in the 18thC and has many fine details, such as the rococo iron gate. Walk round the church to Engels utca, at No. 5 is the Serbian Ecclesiastical Art Museum which has stunning displays of icons and other religious artefacts. The point where Engels utca meets Rákóczi utca is dominated by what is now the Calvinist Church, though it too has older origins. The baroque town hall further down Rákóczi utca is worthy of note though only one wing can be seen from the street – a better view is from Ligeti utca. Along Május I utca there is another large baroque church, the Church of St. Peter. Cutting through the narrow side streets beyond will take you into Hunyadi utca and then back into Fő tér. After exploring Szentendre, follow the signs for Pilisszentlászló northwest out of town and you will come to the open-air ethnographic museum, the Skanzen (see **CHILDREN**). Continue along the Pilisszentlászló road through winding, densely-wooded slopes and keep an eye out for deer and eagles. Beyond Pilisszentlászló you begin your descent down to the Danube. Turn right when you reach Road 11.

36 km – **Visegrád** (see **A-Z**). The administrative centre of the Pilis Park Forest. Visit the reconstructed medieval Royal Palace and admire the views of the river. Solomon's Tower houses finds from excavations in the area (0900-1630 Tue.-Sun., 5 Ft). Retrace your route along Road 11 but continue past the Pilisszentlászló turn-off.

60 km – Esztergom (see **A-Z**). A town which was destroyed by the Turks and reconstructed in the 19thC. It is dominated by the Basilica, the largest church in Hungary. Also of interest are the reconstructed section of the medieval Royal Palace (next to the Basilica) and the Christian Museum at Berényi Zsigmond utca 2. Return along Road 11 towards Budapest. Shortly after Basaharc a left turn down to the river is signposted with the ferry symbol. The ferry docks at Szob on the north bank. Follow Road 12 east through Nagymaros. Admire the view of Visegrád on the south bank. Turn right onto Road 2 by which time the Danube has been divided by Szentendre Island.

95 km – Vác (see **A-Z**). The town is important from a historical and religious viewpoint, and has a baroque feel to it. The triumphal arch and the Town Hall were built to mark the visit of the Empress Maria Theresa in 1764. To return to Budapest the most direct route is along Road 2, though a more scenic route would be to take the ferry from Vác onto Szentendre Island. A bridge at the village of Tahitótfalu links the island with the Pilis bank of the river north of Szentendre and Road 11.

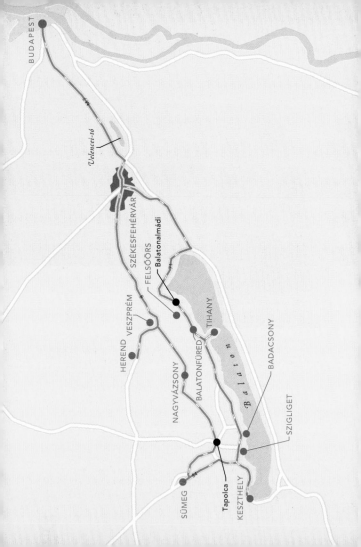

Lake Balaton

A two-day trip to the northern shore of this picturesque lake.

Leave Budapest on the M 7, following the signs for Balaton. Just after passing the smaller lake of Velence (Velencei-tó), turn off the M 7.

70 km – Székesfehérvár. The old centre boasts many fine baroque buildings. Continue along the M 7 and after 27 km turn off on Road 71 to drive around the northern end of Lake Balaton before turning south-west through the busy resort of Balatonalmádi. Just after, take a short detour inland to Felsoörs. The short climb up the hill is a good vantage point from which to view the lake. The main attraction of this settlement is its old church, parts of which date from the 13thC. Return to the lake at Alsóörs.

144 km – Balatonfüred. An important thermal and lakeside resort. The most interesting parts of town lie between the main road and the lake. Continue along the lake and turn left onto the Tihany peninsula.

152 km – Tihany (see A-Z). A village with an imposing 18thC abbey church and museum. Rejoin Road 71 to continue your journey.

206 km – Badacsony. Famous for its wines, this popular summer resort has an impressive backdrop of volcanic mountains and vineyards.

211 km – Szigliget. The village maintains its integrity in spite of the many holiday homes and has an interesting castle and church.

231 km – Keszthely (see A-Z). A good place to spend the night. Try the Helikon Hotel on the shores of the lake. Retrace your route 15 km back along Road 71 and turn left along Road 84.

271 km – Sümeg. This town is dominated by a recently-restored fortress which withstood Turkish attacks. The town was completely destroyed, however, and the buildings date from a later period. Follow signs to Tapolca, winding through the Bakony hills. At Tapolca turn left.

314 km – Nagyvázsony. The picturesque castle dates from the Middle Ages. An outdoor village museum and post office museum can also be visited. One of the small churches dates from the 15thC.

337 km – Veszprém (see A-Z). Another picturesque town, dominated by its castle district, situated on a rocky outcrop. Climb the Fire Tower for an excellent view. Take the main Road 8 in a northwest direction.

351 km – Herend. Notable for its porcelain (see **Best Buys**) which can be admired in the museum next to the factory. Take Road 8 to circle Veszprém and join the M 7 at Székesfehérvár, leading to Budapest.

Pécs Region

A two-day excursion to the main towns in the south of Hungary.
Take the M 7 to Érd and cut across to Road 6, the main Pécs road.
198 km – Pécs. Start your tour in the centre of the old inner city –
Széchenyi tér. In the middle is the former mosque with the crescent of
Islam surmounted by a crucifix signifying its more recent function as a
Catholic church. The mosque itself was built by the Turks in the 16thC.
The Janus Pannonius Museum has an archaeological collection which
outlines the history of the area before the arrival of the Magyars. In
nearby Dóm tér is the impressive cathedral. 19thC reconstruction is
responsible for its present-day facade but its foundations and crypt date
back to the 11thC. Older relics from the Roman period surround the
square and other parts of the Janus Pannonius Museum can be found as
well as the Zsolnay Museum with fine examples of that style of porcelain work. Back down the hill in Rákóczi utca is another mosque, complete with minaret, which dates from the 16thC. Kossuth Lajos utca,
mostly pedestrianized, is the main shopping and commercial street. If
you plan to stay the night the following two centrally-placed hotels can
be recommended: Hotel Pannonia, Rákóczi utca 3 and Hotel Nádor,
Széchenyi tér 15. Take Road 58 south out of the city towards the
Yugoslavian border. After 25 km turn east towards Siklós, passing
through the Villányi area, famed for its wines.
230 km – Siklós. Its 15thC castle was built on the site of a Roman settlement and extensively reconstructed in the 18thC after 143 years of
Turkish occupation. It is now a hotel. The Prison Museum it houses is
fairly gory and not recommended to the weak of stomach. The Gothic
chapel features some nice stone carvings. Follow directions to Villány
and continue east, winding through some pleasant country roads.
265 km – Mohács. The memorial park to the south of the town has
some interesting wooden statues which mark the defeat of the
Hungarian army by the Turks on this site in 1526. The Votive Church in
Széchenyi tér was built to mark the 400th anniversary of this massacre
and the town museum provides exhibits from the battlefield. The town
is also famous for its celebrations of the coming of spring in February –
Carnival Sunday sees a procession of colourfully-dressed locals, some
of whom wear masks. Road 56 takes you north along the Danube
through Szekszárd and onto Road 6, leading back to Budapest.

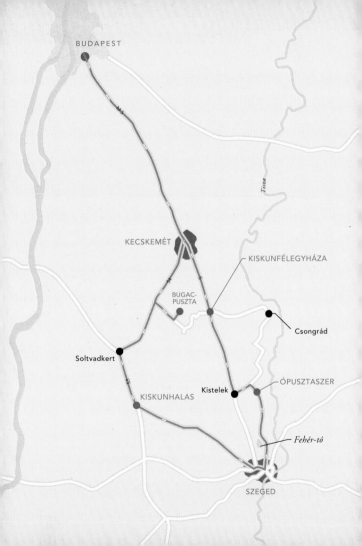

The Great Plain

A two-day exploration of the central and eastern region of Hungary.
Leave Budapest by following the signs for Szeged on the M 5.

85 km – Kecskemét (see **A-Z**). A market town and thriving agricultural
centre, it boasts many original examples of the style that became
known as New Hungarian. The Kecskemét Gallery at Rákóczi utca 1
has a collection of works by contemporary Hungarian artists. 1000-
1800 Tue.-Sun. (1700 winter), entry 5 Ft. Road 54 takes you through
the Kiskunság region, some of which forms part of the National Park.

125 km – Bugac-Puszta. This lies in an area where traditional methods
of agriculture have been preserved. There is a Pastoral Life Museum
and regular displays by the Csikós or Hungarian Cowboys. Back on
Road 54, continue southwest to Soltvadkert and join Road 53.

173 km – Kiskunhalas. Famous for its lace. The Lace House, a working
museum, stands where Road 53 meets Kossuth Lajos utca. In Kölcsey
utca you can see the last of the 90 windmills that used to operate in the
area. Take the Szeged road, which improves in quality as you go along.

233 km – Szeged (see **A-Z**). Built on the River Tisza, this important cultural, administrative and university centre was largely destroyed by
flooding in 1879. Of the pre-flood buildings, the Serbian Church is
interesting, but most of the town has been rebuilt. Visit the impressive
Votive Church with its twin towers. Of the three main hotels the
Hungaria (three-star) is the most modern, the Tisza (two-star) is run-
down but in a grand building, and the Royal is centrally located. It is
essential to book if you come here during the summer Theatre Festival.
From Szeged follow the signs for Csongrád, passing Fehér-tó (White
Lake), a large fish farm/nature reserve. This is on migratory routes for
over 250 species of bird – resident in the summer are herons and egret
and the ubiquitous white stork can be seen on the chimney-tops.

262 km – Ópusztaszer. The site of the first assembly of the seven
Magyar tribal chieftains responsible for founding the nation in AD 896.
A large crowd gathers here on the 20th August for Constitution Day.
Follow signs left towards the main Budapest/Szeged road.

302 km – Kiskunfélegyháza. Boasts a grand Town Hall, completed in
1912, and a small museum housed in the former Cumarnion Captain's
House at Vörös Hadsereg utca 9. Head northwards on Road 5 which
will take you back through Kecskemét to Budapest.

VÁROSLIGET

ARANY SAS
PATIKAMÚZEUM

Városház u.

SEMMELWEIS
ORVOSTÖRTÉNETI
MÚZEUM

Erzsébet krt.

Teréz krt.   Andrássy út.

ÖNTÖDEI
MÚZEUM

Kossuth
Lajos
tér

KERESKEDELMI ÉS
VENDÉGLÁTÓIPARI
MÚZEUM

GELLÉRTHEGY

Danube

Apród u.

BUDAPESTI TÖRTÉNETI MÚZEUM

MAGYAR
NEMZETI
GALÉRIA

AQUINCUMI
MÚZEUM

Várhegy

HADTÖRTÉNETI
MÚZEUM

Buda

MAGYAR NEMZETI GALÉRIA I, Király palota, Wings B, C, & D.
❏ 1000-1800 Tue.-Sun. Funicular railway from Clark Ádám tér. ❏ 10 Ft.
Hungary's national collection, featuring Hungarian painters and sculp-tors from medieval times to the present day. See **A-Z**.

BUDAPESTI TÖRTÉNETI MÚZEUM I, Király palota, Wing E.
❏ 1000-1800 Tue.-Sun. Funicular railway from Clark Ádám tér. ❏ 10 Ft.
The historical museum, relating Budapest's turbulent past. Many of the exhibits here were found on Castle Hill. See **A-Z**.

KERESKEDELMI ÉS VENDÉGLÁTÓIPARI MÚZEUM
I, Fortuna u. 4.
❏ 1000-1800 Tue.-Sun. Bus 16, 16A.
Artefacts of the old catering industry in Hungary and some interesting (and genuine) set-pieces. See **WALK 2**, **A-Z**.

HADTÖRTÉNETI MÚZEUM I, Tóth Árpád sétány 40.
❏ 0900-1700 Tue.-Sat, 1000-1800 Sun. Bus 16, 16A. ❏ 10 Ft.
Military artefacts, weaponry and uniforms. See **WALK 2**, **A-Z**.

ARANY SAS PATIKAMÚZEUM I, Tárnok u. 18.
❏ 1030-1730 Tue.-Sun. Bus 16, 16A. ❏ 6 Ft.
Pharmaceutical preparations and surgical instruments. See **WALK 2**.

AQUINCUMI MÚZEUM III, Szentendrei út 139.
❏ 1000-1600 Tue.-Sun. HÉV from Batthyány tér to Aquincum. ❏ 10 Ft.
Exhibits of sculptures, ceramics, coins, jewellery, etc. give an insight into the Roman settlement. See **CITY SIGHTS 2**, **Aquincum**.

SEMMELWEIS ORVOSTÖRTÉNETI MÚZEUM I, Apród u. 1-3.
❏ 1030-1730 Tue.-Sun. Bus 5, 78, 86; Tram 9, 19. ❏ 6 Ft.
Displays illustrating the development of medicine. See **A-Z**.

ÖNTÖDEI MÚZEUM II, Bem Jószef u. 20.
❏ 0900-1500 Mon., 0900-1600 Tue.-Sun. Bus 12, 12A, 84; Tram 4, 6.
Housed in a foundry, a museum about the history of metal casting.

NEMZETI MÚZEUM V, Múzeum krt. 14-16.
❑ 1000-1800 Tue.-Sun. Bus 1, 9; M Kálvin tér. ❑ 10 Ft (free Wed.).
The history of Hungary from prehistoric times up to the mid-18thC, the main attraction being the Crown Jewels. See WALK 1, **A-Z**.

NÉPRAJZI MÚZEUM V, Kossuth Lajos tér 12.
❑ 1000-1800 Tue.-Sun. Bus 15; Tram 2, 2A; M Kossuth tér. ❑ 10 Ft.
Ethnographical material – jewellery, religious art, etc. See WALK 1, **A-Z**.

SZÉPMŰVÉSZETI MÚZEUM XIV, Dózsa György út 41.
❑ 1000-1715 Tue.-Sun. M Hosök tere. ❑ 10 Ft (free Sat.).
Egyptian statuary, Greek ceramics, and European art. See **A-Z**.

IPARMŰVÉSZETI MÚZEUM IX, Üllői út 33-37.
❑ 1000-1800 Tue.-Sun. Bus 182; M Ferenc krt. ❑ 5 Ft.
The history and techniques of a wide variety of arts and crafts. See **A-Z**.

HOPP FERENC MÚZEUM VI, Andrássy út 103.
❑ 1000-1800 Tue.-Sun. Bus 1, 4, 4A; M Bajza utca. ❑ 5 Ft.
20,000 items from the Indian subcontinent and the Far East. See **A-Z**.

KINA MÚZEUM VI, Gorkij fasor 12.
❑ 1000-1800 Tue.-Sun. Bus 33; Trolleybus 70, 78. ❑ 5 Ft (free Sat.).
A collection of art, sculpture and ceramics from China and Japan.

ZSIDÓ MÚZEUM VII, Dohány u. 2.
❑ 1000-1800 Tue.-Sun. Bus 1, 9; Tram 47, 49; M Astoria. ❑ 5 Ft.
The development of the Jewish religion in Hungary. See **A-Z**.

PÓSTAMÚZEUM VI, Andrássy út 3 (first floor).
❑ 1000-1800 Tue.-Sun. Bus 1, 4, 4A; M Bajcsy-Zsilinsky út. ❑ 5 Ft.
An interesting history of postal services and telecommunications.

KÖZLEKEDÉSI MÚZEUM XIV, Városligeti krt. 11.
❑ 1000-1800 Wed.-Sun. Trolleybus 70, 72. ❑ 10 Ft (free Wed.).
Insights into modes of transport on rail, road and water through the ages.

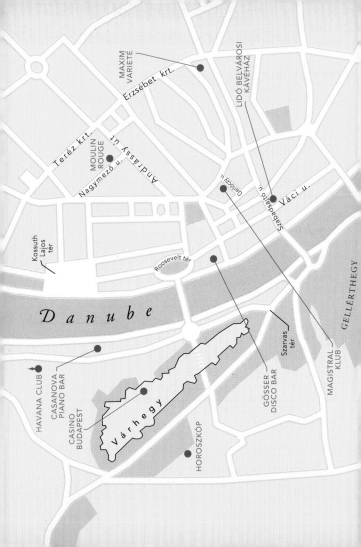

MAXIM
VARIETÉ

LIDÓ BELVÁROSI
KÁVÉHÁZ

Erzsébet krt.

Teréz krt.

MOULIN
ROUGE

Nagymező u.

Andrássy u.

Gerlóczy u.

Szabadsajtó u.

Váci u.

Kossuth
Lajos
tér

Roosevelt tér

D a n u b e

GELLÉRTHEGY

Szarvas
tér

HAVANA CLUB

CASANOVA
PIANO BAR

CASINO
BUDAPEST

V á r h e g y

GÖSSER
DISCO BAR

MAGISTRAL
KLUB

HOROSZKÓP

CASINO BUDAPEST Hilton Hotel: I, Hess András tér 1-3.
❑ 1700-0200. Bus 16, 16A. ❑ 10 DM.
Formal dress, hard currency and passport required.

CASANOVA PIANO BAR I, Batthyány tér 4.
❑ 2200-0500. Bus 60, 86; Tram 9, 19; M Batthyány tér.
Modern cocktails and soft piano music playing in the background.

GÖSSER DISCO BAR V, Szende Pál u. 1.
❑ 1200-0300 (disco 2300-0300). Bus 2, 15. ❑ Disco 100 Ft.
Popular with tourists. Good cocktails and pop music.

HAVANA CLUB Thermal Hotel: XIII, Margitsziget.
❑ 2200-0200 Mon.-Sat. Bus 26. ❑ 250 Ft.
Show by Cuban artists at 2400 daily. Reservations advisable.

HOROSZKÓP Buda Penta Hotel: I, Krisztina krt. 41-43.
❑ 2200-0400, floorshow at 2300. Bus 18. ❑ 200 Ft (incl. one drink).
Fashionable disco playing pop music. Snacks served. Advisable to book.

LIDÓ BELVÁROSI KÁVÉHÁZ V, Szabadsajtó u. 5.
❑ 1000-0400. M Felszabadulás. ❑ 700 Ft (inc. drink), 500 Ft (no drink).
Popular nightclub with floor shows and gipsy/folk music and dancing.

MAGISTRAL KLUB V, Gerlóczy u. 4.
❑ 2100-dawn Mon.-Sat. Bus 1, 9; M Deák Ferenc tér.
A very popular nightspot where you can dance till dawn to loud music.

MAXIM VARIETÉ VII, Akácfa u. 3.
❑ 1930-0230. Bus 7, 7A, 78. ❑ 1450 Ft (inc. dinner),1050 (no dinner).
Floorshow and dancing – admission easier for tourists than locals.

MOULIN ROUGE VI, Nagymező u. 17.
❑ 2000-0300. Trolleybus 70, 78. ❑ 1300 Ft (inc. dinner and drink).
Revue-type show and orchestra with dancing. Reservations in advance.

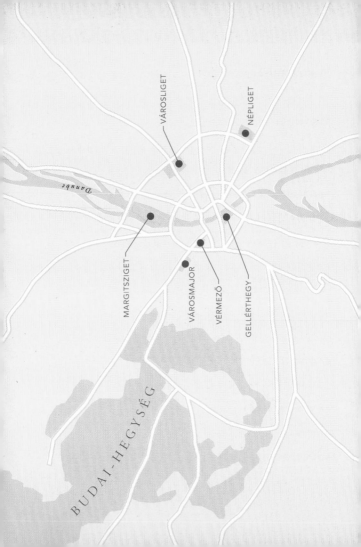

VÁROSLIGET

NÉPLIGET

Danube

MARGITSZIGET

VÁROSMAJOR

VÉRMEZŐ

GELLÉRTHEGY

BUDAI-HEGYSÉG

MARGITSZIGET (MARGARET ISLAND)
Via Árpád híd or Margit híd. Bus 26.
A 2.5 km-long island between Pest and Buda that has been made into a recreation and sports centre with hotels and various attractions. See **A-Z**.

VÁROSLIGET (CITY PARK)
Bus 1, 4, 4A, 20, 30; Trolleybus 70, 72, 74, 75; M Hősök tere.
250 acres of parkland attracting visitors for bathing, boating, and therapeutic baths, as well as the zoo and fun fair. See **CHILDREN**, **WALK 3**, **A-Z**.

GELLÉRTHEGY (GELLÉRT HILL)
Bus 27.
Approximately 230 m above sea level, Gellért Hill offers wonderful views of the city and the Danube. It is the site of the Citadella (see **BUILDINGS**, **A-Z***) and the Szabadság szobor, or Liberation Monument (see* **CITY SIGHTS 1**, **A-Z***). See* **A-Z**.

VÉRMEZŐ (BLOOD FIELD)
Bus 5; Tram 18, 49; M Déli pályaudvar.
Pleasant shady park with children's play area. Ideal for a picnic or a rest.

VÁROSMAJOR (MUNICIPAL GROUNDS)
Bus 5, 22, 56; M Moszkva tér.
A small park with some beautiful old trees near the terminus of the cogwheel railway. A modern Roman Catholic church stands nearby.

NÉPLIGET (PEOPLE'S PARK)
Bus 55, 182; Trolleybus 75; M Népliget.
A modern park which has several areas reserved for a variety of sports and is particularly popular with joggers.

BUDAI-HEGYSÉG (BUDA HILLS)
Bus 28, 57, 63, 64, 157, 164, 190; cog-wheel railway from Városmajor to Széchenyi-hegy.
Desirable residential area with plenty of opportunities for gentle walking, wildlife spotting and good views from Jánoshegy. See **A-Z**.

GUNDEL

VÁROSLIGET

Állatkerti út

LÉGRÁDI TESTVÉREK

Erzsébet krt.

Teréz krt.

Andrássy út

MÁTYÁS PINCE

Kossuth Lajos tér

MARCO POLO

Belgrád

GELLÉRTHEGY

Danube

SZÁZÉVES

ARANYHORDÓ

PÓSTAKOCSI

ALABÁRDOS

KALOCSA

Várhegy

RESTAURANTS 1

ALABÁRDOS I, Országház u. 2.
❑ 1900-2400 Mon.-Sat. Bus 16, 16A.
Essential to reserve in this small, medieval-type Castle District restaurant. Fish and game specialities, and the music is never too intrusive.

ARANYHORDÓ I, Tárnok u. 16.
❑ 1200-2400. Bus 16, 16A.
Excellent Hungarian cuisine accompanied by lively gipsy music.

GUNDEL XIV, Állatkerti út 2.
❑ 1200-1600, 1900-2400. Trolleybus 72; M Széchenyifürdő.
Named after the chef and food writer who first owned it.

KALOCSA Hilton Hotel: I, Hess András tér 1-3.
❑ 1200-1600, 1900-2400. Bus 16, 16A.
The service and quality of food is as expected in this prestigious hotel.

LÉGRÁDI TESTVÉREK V, Magyar u. 23.
❑ 1900-2400 Mon.-Fri. Bus 1, 9; M Kálvin tér or Astoria.
Excellent Hungarian and French cuisine. Popular with the locals.

MARCO POLO V, Vigadó tér 3.
❑ 1200-1500, 1930-2400 Mon.-Sat. Bus 2, 15; M Vörösmarty tér.
Italian restaurant that has rapidly acquired a reputation for excellence.

MÁTYÁS PINCE V, Március 15 tér 7.
❑ 1200-1500, 1900-2400. Bus 5, 8, 8A; M Felszabadulás tér.
Hungarian cuisine accompanied by an excellent gipsy orchestra.

PÓSTAKOCSI III, Fő tér 2.
❑ 1200-2400. Bus 18, 37, 42, 134, 137, 142.
Essential to reserve in advance in this Óbuda borozo (wine-bar).

SZÁZÉVES V, Pesti Barnabás u. 2.
❑ 1200-2400. Bus 5, 8, 8A; M Felszabulás tér.
Game and fish specialities available in this long-established restaurant.

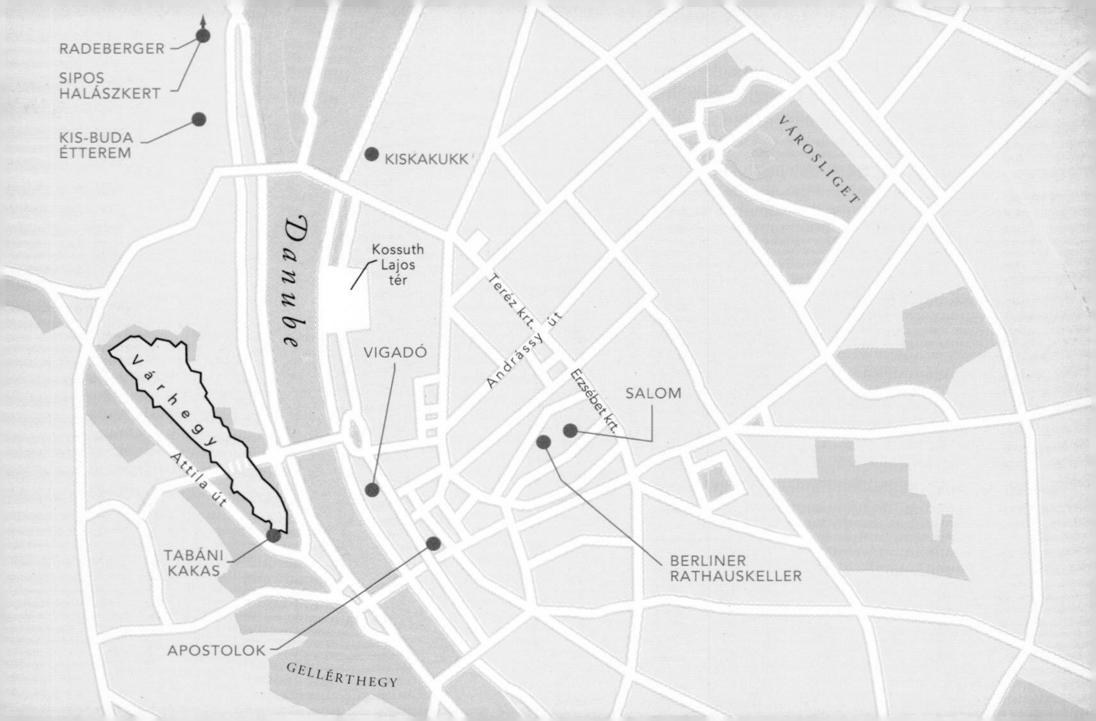

VÁROSLIGET

BERLINER
RATHAUSKELLER

SALOM

Erzsébet krt.

Andrássy út

Teréz krt.

KISKAKUKK

Kossuth
Lajos
tér

VIGADÓ

GELLÉRTHEGY

Danube

Várhegy

APOSTOLOK

Attila út

TABÁNI
KAKAS

RADEBERGER

SIPOS
HALÁSZKERT

KIS-BUDA
ÉTTEREM

Moderate

APOSTOLOK V, Kígyó u. 4-6.
❏ 1200-2400. Bus 2, 5, 7, 7A, 112; M Felszabadulás tér.
A somewhat spartan atmosphere enlivened by stained-glass

BERLINER RATHAUSKELLER VII, Dob u. 31, entry Kazinczy u.
❏ 1200-2300 Mon.-Sat, 1800-2300 Sun. Closed Sun. (Oct.-April).
A good selection of beers and Hungarian and international cuisine.

KIS-BUDA ÉTTEREM II, Frankel Leó u. 34.
❏ 1200-2400 Mon.-Sat., 1200-1500 Sun. Bus 42, 60, 86; Tram 17.
Piano and violin accompany excellent food. Good selection of wines.

KISKAKUKK XIII, Pozsonyi út 12.
❏ 1200-2300 Mon.-Sat., 1200-1600 Sun. Closed Sun. (summer).
Trolleybus 76, 79.
Popular in spite of uninspired decor – game dishes are particularly good.

RADEBERGER III, Hídfő u. 16.
❏ 1200-2400. Bus 18, 37, 42, 134, 137, 142.
Gipsy music accompanies the Hungarian and international dishes.

SALOM VII, Klauzál tér 2.
❏ 1200-2000 Mon.-Fri. (2200 summer), 1100-1500 Sat. Trolleybus 74.
One of the few kosher restaurants in the city. The food is excellent.

SIPOS HALÁSZKERT III, Fő tér 6.
❏ 1200-2400. Bus 18, 37, 42, 134, 137, 142.
Óbuda restaurant offering fish specialities and Hungarian folk music.

TABÁNI KAKAS I, Attila út 7.
❏ 1200-2400 Mon.-Fri., 1300-2400 Sat., Sun. Bus 5.
Popular restaurant specializing in game dishes as well as pork and veal.

VIGADÓ V, Vigadó tér.
❏ 1200-2400. Bus 2, 15; Tram 2, 2A; M Vörösmarty tér.
Excellent service with good Hungarian food and beer on the menu.

GÖRÖG TAVERNA

Erzsébet krt.

BOHÉMTANYA

KISPIPA

Teréz krt.

Andrássy út

Dob u.

ARANYPINCE

ALFÖLDI

Kecskeméti u.

Váci u.

Bécsi u.

Kossuth
Lajos
tér

Roosevelt tér

Danube

GELLÉRTHEGY

NÁDUDVAR
ÉTELBÁR

Szarvas
tér

RÉZKAKAS

TIROLI

Várhegy

Inexpensive

ARANYPINCE VII, Dob u. 6.
❏ 1200-2300 Mon.-Sat., 1200-2200 Sun. Bus 1, 9; Tram 47, 49.
Cellar restaurant serving great soups – popular with the locals.

ALFÖLDI V, Kecskeméti u. 4.
❏ 1100-2400. Bus 15; M Kálvin tér.
Hungarian cuisine. Very busy at lunchtime so be prepared to queue. In summer there are tables outside, if you can take the exhaust fumes.

BOHÉMTANYA VI, Paulay Ede u. 6.
❏ 1100-2200. Bus 1, 4, 4A; M Bajcsy-Zsilinszky út.
Popular at peak times but the food is worth the wait. Imaginative cooking with at least one vegetarian dish on the menu. Friendly service.

GÖRÖG TAVERNA VII, Csengery u. 24.
❏ 1200-0200. Bus 12, 12A; Tram 4, 6.
Greek restaurant in a cellar serving lovingly-prepared dishes accompanied by Greek music.

KISPIPA VII, Akácfa u. 38.
❏ 1200-0100 Mon.-Sat. Bus 12, 12A; Tram 4, 6; Trolleybus 74.
The fish and poultry dishes have deservedly acquired an excellent reputation. Very popular and advance booking is essential. Piano music.

NÁDUDVAR ÉTELBÁR V, Bécsi u.
❏ 1000-1900 Mon.-Fri. Bus 15; M Vörösmarty tér.
Good Hungarian cooking, quick service with places to eat at counter.

RÉZKAKAS V, Veres Pálné u. 3.
❏ 1100-2300 Mon.-Sat., 1100-1500 Sun. M Felszabadulás tér.
Poultry dishes and soups are the specialities of the house here.

TIROLI II, Lajos u. 33.
❏ 1200-2400 Mon.-Sat., 1200-1500 Sun. Bus 6, 42, 60, 84, 86.
Veal specialities and dishes from the Tyrol region. It is advisable to book at least one day in advance.

Párizsi udvar, Felszabadulás tér

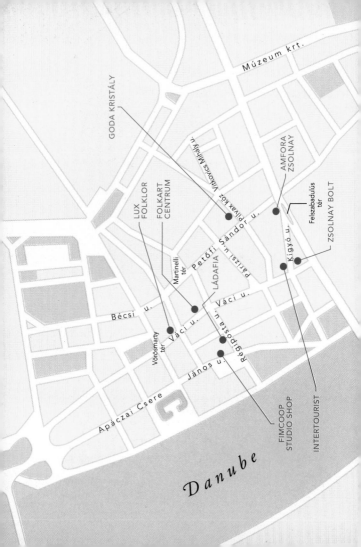

Múzeum krt.

GODA KRISTÁLY

AMFORA
ZSOLNAY

Vitkovics Mihály u.

Felszabadulás
tér

ZSOLNAY BOLT

LUX
FOLKLOR

FOLKART
CENTRUM

Kígyó u.

Pilvax köz

Petőfi Sándor u.

Martinelli
tér

LÁDAFIA

párizsi u.

Bécsi   u.

Váci u.

Váci u.

Régiposta u.

Vörösmarty
tér

János u.

Apáczai Csere u.

FIMCOOP
STUDIO SHOP

INTERTOURIST

Danube

Crafts

FOLKART CENTRUM V, Váci u. 14.
❑ 0930-1800 Mon.-Wed., Fri., 0930-1900 Thu., 0930-1700 Sat., 0930-1400 Sun. Bus 2, 15.
Large shop selling a wide range of embroidery, pottery, rugs and carpets.

LÁDAFIA V, Régipósta u. 6.
❑ 1000-1800 Mon.-Fri, 0930-1330 Sat. Bus 2, 15.
Behind the Folkart Centrum and more intimate. Wonderful embroidery.

LUX FOLKLOR V, Váci u. 6.
❑ 0930-1830. Bus 2, 15.
Small shop, privately-owned and selling high-quality goods.

AMFORA ZSOLNAY V, Felszabadulás tér 4.
❑ 1000-1800 Mon.-Fri. M Felszabadulás tér.
Part of a chain offering a good selection of Zsolnay tableware.

ZSOLNAY BOLT V, Kígyó u. 4.
❑ 0900-1800 Mon.-Wed., Fri., 0900-2000 Thu., 0900.-1300 Sat.
Bus 5, 7, 7A; M Felszabadulás tér.
Perhaps the largest selection of Zsolnay porcelain in Budapest.

GODA KRISTÁLY V, Pilvax köz 1.
❑ 1000-1800 Mon.-Wed., Fri., 1000-1900 Thu., 1000-1300 Sat.
Bus 2, 15; M Felszabadulás tér.
Gilded and coloured crystal – glasses, vases, decanters and bowls. A bit too much for some tastes.

INTERTOURIST V, Kígyó u. 5 (and at many other sales points).
❑ 1000-1800 Mon.-Fri., 0900-1300 Sat. Bus 5, 7, 7A; M Felszabadulás.
A wide range of Hungarian crafts. Only hard currency accepted.

FIMCOOP STUDIO SHOP V, Apáczai Csere János u. 7.
❑ 1000-1800 Mon.-Fri. Bus 2, 15.
*Worth a visit for its range of good-quality Herend porcelain (see **Best Buys**) and Hollóháza and Zsolnay items. Figurines as well as tableware.*

PÁRIZSI TANGÓ RÉGISÉG BOLT

BELVÁROSI ANTIQUITAS

Múzeum krt.

ANTIQUITAS

QUALITAS GALÉRIA

Vitkovics Mihály u.

Pilvax köz

Váci köz

Petőfi Sándor u.

Párizsi u.

Kigyó u.

Felszabadulás tér

KÖZPONTI ANTIKVÁRIUM

ZENEI ANTIKVÁRIUM

Martinelli tér

Bécsi u.

Vörösmarty tér

Váci u.

Váci u.

Regiposta u.

Apáczai Csere János u.

QUALITAS ANTIQUITAS

GALÉRIA

ANTIKVÁRIUM

Danube

ANTIQUITAS V, Bécsi u. 1-3.
❑ 1000-1800 Mon.-Wed., Fri., 1000-1900 Thu., 0900-1300 Sat. Bus 2.
Two sections – one dealing with furniture, sculpture, mirrors, etc. and the other with jewellery, figurines, and smaller objects.

PÁRIZSI TANGÓ RÉGISÉG BOLT V, Párizsi u. 6/b.
❑ 1000-1800 Mon.-Fri., 1000-1300 Sat. Bus 2, 15.
A small shop with a surprisingly varied and interesting range of antiques.

QUALITAS ANTIQUITAS V, Néphadsereg u. 32.
❑ 1000-1800 Mon.-Fri, 1000-1300 Sat. Tram 2, 2A.
Owned by an enthusiast, expert and author on the subject of antiques.

ANTIKVÁRIUM V, Váci u. 28.
❑ 1000-1800 Mon.-Fri., 0930-1300 Sat. Bus 2, 15.
Relatively recent publications can be found amongst the old books.

KÖZPONTI ANTIKVÁRIUM V, Múzeum krt. 15.
❑ 1000-1800 Mon.-Fri., 1000-1300 Sat. Bus 1, 9; Tram 47, 49.
Largest shop dealing in second-hand books and a nice selection of maps.

ZENEI ANTIKVÁRIUM V, Múzeum krt. 17-21.
❑ 1000-1800 Mon.-Fri., 1000-1300 Sat. Bus 1, 9; Tram 47, 49.
Music books, sheet music and recordings of classical works.

GALÉRIA V, Petőfi Sándor u. 18.
❑ 1000-1800 Mon.-Fri., 1000-1300 Sat. Bus 2, 15.
Art gallery dealing mainly in graphic art. Etchings are the speciality.

QUALITAS GALÉRIA V, Bécsi u. 2.
❑ 1000-1800 Mon.-Fri., 1000-1300 Sat. Bus 2, 15.
Small gallery dealing in modern art. Sculptures, paintings by local artists.

BELVÁROSI ANTIQUITAS V, Vitkovics Mihály u. 3.
❑ 1000-1800 Mon.-Fri., 1000-1400 Sat. Bus 1, 9; Tram 47, 49.
Antique shop with an interesting collection of artefacts. Helpful staff.

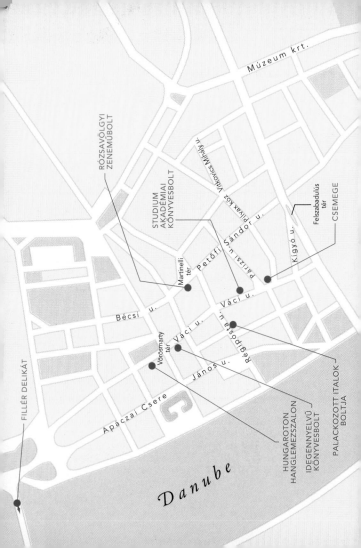

RÓZSAVÖLGYI
ZENEMŰBOLT

STUDIUM
AKADÉMIAI
KÖNYVESBOLT

Múzeum krt.

Vitkovics Mihály u.

Pilvax köz

Párizsi u.

Felszabadulás
tér

CSEMEGE

Kigyó u.

Martinelli
tér

Petőfi Sándor u.

Váci u.

Bécsi u.

Váci u.

Régiposta u.

Vörösmarty
tér

János u.

Apáczai Csere

FILLÉR DELIKÁT

HUNGAROTON
HANGLEMEZSZALON

IDEGENNYELVŰ
KÖNYVESBOLT

PALACKOZOTT ITALOK
BOLTJA

Danube

STUDIUM AKADÉMIAI KÖNYVESBOLT V, Váci u. 22.
❑ 1000-1800 Mon.-Wed., Fri., 1000-1900 Thu., 0900-1300 Sat. Bus 2.
Good selection of travel guides, cookbooks and other publications aimed at the tourist market.

IDEGENNYELVŰ KÖNYVESBOLT V, Váci u. 32.
❑ 1000-1800 Mon.-Wed., Fri., 1000-2000 Thu., 0900-1300 Sat. Bus 2.
Bookshop specializing in foreign-language publications. Varied selection of paperbacks, maps, travel guides and the usual Hungarian offerings.

PALACKOZOTT ITALOK BOLTJA V, Régiposta u. 11.
❑ 1000-1800 Mon.-Fri., 1000-1300 Sat. Bus 2, 15.
A wide range and varied selection of Hungarian wines with the owners, who speak German and some English, always ready to help you choose. Also sells other Hungarian produce.

FILLÉR DELIKÁT II, Retek u. 6.
❑ 1000-1800 Mon.-Fri., 1000-1300 Sat. M Moszkva tér.
Sells imported drinks and other goodies as well as Hungarian produce such as chocolate liqueur cherries and goose-liver pâté. Also individual bottles of Tokaji (see **Drinks**).

CSEMEGE V, Váci u. 3.
❑ 0700-2000 Mon.-Fri., 0800-1500 Sat. Bus 2, 15.
A supermarket (one of a chain) offering a good selection of food and drink – interesting to see what sort of merchandise is on general sale.

HUNGAROTON HANGLEMEZSZALON V, Vörösmarty tér.
❑ 0930-1800 Mon.-Fri., 1000-1700 Sat. Bus 2, 15; M Vörösmarty tér.
Helpful German- and English-speaking staff selling all kinds of music at reasonable prices. There is a good selection of Hungarian artists on CD.

RÓZSAVÖLGYI ZENEMŰBOLT V, Martinelli tér 5.
❑ 0930-1800 Mon., Wed., Fri., 0900-1800 Tue., 1930-2000 Thu., 0900-1330 Sat. Bus 2, 15.
A wide collection of records, cassettes and music books.

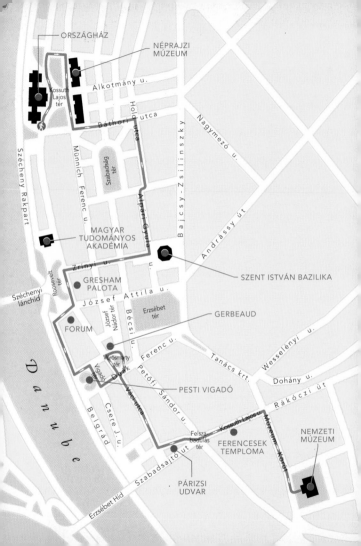

ORSZÁGHÁZ

NÉPRAJZI MÚZEUM

Alkotmány u.

Kossuth Lajos tér

Hold utca

Báthori utca

Széchenyi Rakpart

Münnich Ferenc u.

Szabadság tér

Alpári Gyula u.

Bajcsy-Zsilinszky u.

Nagymező u.

Andrássy út

MAGYAR TUDOMÁNYOS AKADÉMIA

Zrínyi u.

SZENT ISTVÁN BAZILIKA

Roosevelt tér

GRESHAM PALOTA

József Attila u.

Széchenyi lánchíd

FORUM

József tér

Bécsi u.

Nádor tér

Erzsébet tér

GERBEAUD

Danube

Vörösmarty tér

Deák

Ferenc u.

Tanács krt.

Wesselényi u.

Vigadó

Dorottya u.

Petőfi Sándor u.

Vármegye u.

PESTI VIGADÓ

Dohány u.

Rákóczi út

Belgrád

Csere J. u.

Váci utca

Felszabadulás tér

Kossuth Lajos u.

Múzeum körút

NEMZETI MÚZEUM

Erzsébet Híd

Szabadsajtó út

PÁRIZSI UDVAR

FERENCESEK TEMPLOMA

Pest Centre

Approximately 2 hr 30 min, not
including stops.
Begin the walk at Kossuth Lajos tér,
which can be reached by Metro or
Tram 2 or 2A. Just to the south of
the Parliament building (see **BUILD-
INGS**, **Országház**) is a small park in
which there is a statue of Attila
József (the 20thC Hungarian poet)
by László Márton (1980). There is
also a statue of Ferenc Rákóczi II
(1676-1735), leader of the anti-
Hapsburg War of Independence
(1703-11). The limestone
Parliament building was completed
in 1902 and contains 200 rooms
including the offices for the
Presidential Council and the Prime
Minister. To the north is a monument of the standing figure of Lajos
Kossuth (1802-94), leader of the

1848-49 Hungarian War of Independence – a well-loved figure who
was elected Governor of Hungary. In front of the north facade of the
Parliament building is a statue of Mihály Károlyi (1875-1955), president
of the Hungarian Republic from 1918-19, by Imre Varga (1975).
Opposite the building, on the east side, are the Ethnographical Museum
(see **MUSEUMS 2**, **Néprajzi Múzeum**) and the Ministry of Agriculture and
Food.
Turn left into Báthory utca as far as Hold utca and you will come to a
small square. An eternal flame burns in memory of Count Lajos
Batthyány who was executed on this spot on 6 October 1849. Many a
demonstration has started here and it was used, as a Berlin metro station, during filming for the BBC series *Christobel*.
Continue along Hold utca and then Alpári Gyula utca which will bring
you to the Basilica or St. Stephen's Church (see **CHURCHES**, **Szent István
bazilika**). Take Zrínyi utca to arrive at Roosevelt tér (see **A-Z**). The

square is surrounded by grand hotels, the Hungarian Academy of Sciences (Magyar Tudományos Akadémia) and, on the east side, the Art Nouveau building called the Gresham Palace, finished in 1906 by Zsigmond Quittner. This square forms the Pest end of the Széchenyi lánchíd (Chain Bridge). Walk south along the river on the Duna Corso, past the Forum Hotel. This is a favourite pastime of the locals, mainly because of the superb view of the Castle District and the river. Just before reaching the Hotel Duna Intercontinental, one comes to Vigadó tér – bordered on the east side by the Pesti Vigadó (see **CULTURE**). The Vigadó was built to the plans of Friggs Freszl between 1859-64 and the statues decorating the facade are by Károly Alexy.

Leaving the river, Deák Ferenc utca will take you into Vörösmarty tér (see **A-Z**). On the north side of the square is the famous Gerbeaud Confectioner's (see **CAFÉS**). Take the exit to the south side of the square and you will find yourself in the pedestrianized Váci utca which is the most popular shopping street in Budapest (see **SHOPPING**). Watch out

Magyar Tudományos Akadémia

Gresham-palota

for pickpockets around here. Many buildings along this street are of interest. No. 9 used to be the *Inn of the Seven Electors* where Liszt (see **A–Z**) performed at the age of eleven. It now houses a theatre company. The facade at No. 11 is decorated by coloured ceramic tiles from Zsolnay. Turn left into Kígyó utca and on your right you will see an elaborate cast-iron gateway leading into the Párizsi udvar (Paris yard) which was built as a shopping arcade in 1911 by Henrik Schmal. If you walk through the arcade you will come out on Felszabadulás tér. Cross to the southeast side via the subway and take a look at the Franciscan Church (see **CHURCHES**, **Ferencesek Temploma**). Continue along Kossuth Lajos utca and cross over Múzeum körút (using the subway) to finish the walk at the Hungarian National Museum (see **MUSEUMS 2**, **Nemzeti Múzeum**). It was built in 1837-47 by Mihály Pollack. On 15 March 1848 Sándor Petőfi (1823-49) recited his *National Song* and the *Twelve Points* from the steps of this building, summing up the demands of the radical intellectuals of the time.

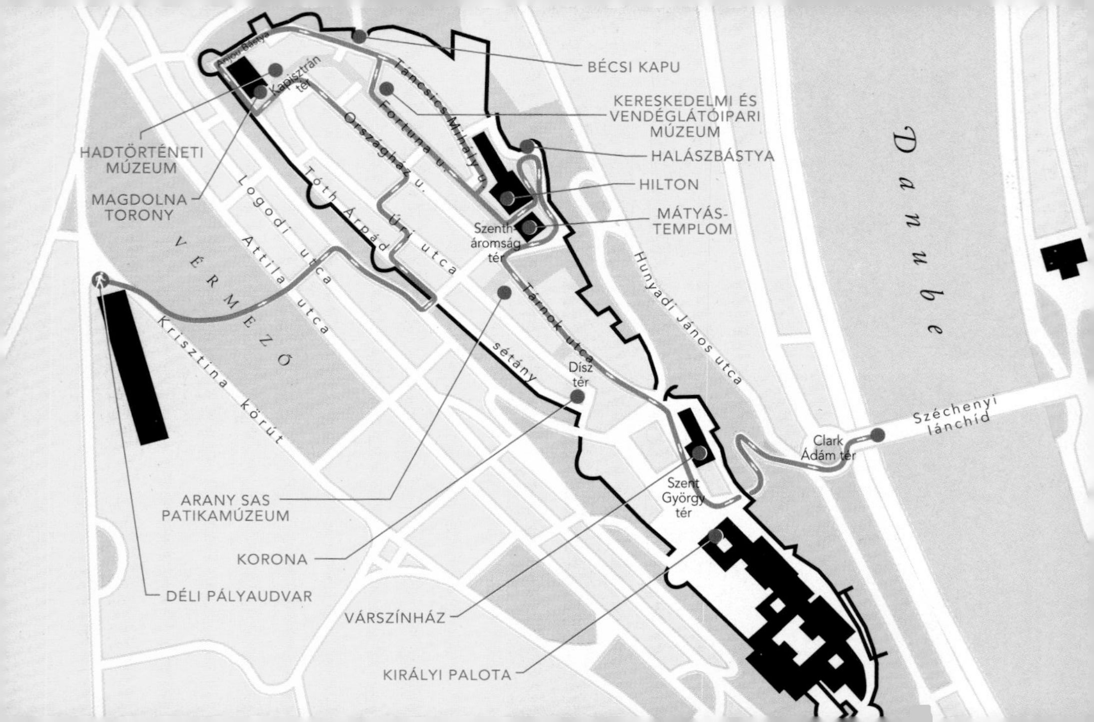

Danube

Széchenyi lánchíd

Clark Ádám tér

BÉCSI KAPU

KERESKEDELMI ÉS VENDÉGLÁTÓIPARI MÚZEUM

HALÁSZBÁSTYA

HILTON

MÁTYÁS-TEMPLOM

Hunyadi János utca

Szent György tér

Tanácsics Mihály u.

Fortuna u.

Országház u.

Úri utca

Szentháromság tér

Tárnok utca

Dísz tér

sétány

Tóth Árpád sétány

Logodi utca

Attila utca

VÉRMEZŐ

Krisztina körút

HADTÖRTÉNETI MÚZEUM

MAGDOLNA TORONY

ARANY SAS PATIKAMÚZEUM

KORONA

DÉLI PÁLYAUDVAR

VÁRSZÍNHÁZ

KIRÁLYI PALOTA

The Castle District

Approximately 3 hr.

From Déli pályaudvar (Southern Railway Station), the most modern of Budapest's stations, take the subway under Krisztina körút which will put you on the right path through Vérmező (see **PARKS**) to Attila utca. After crossing Attila utca go up the steps on Bugát utca and continue over Logodi utca and up the next flight of steps until you come to the staircase leading to the top – opposite the end of Gránit lépcső. On the way up you have passed some of the most desirable residences in the city. The most strenuous part of the walk is now over and you will probably want to stop and admire the marvellous panorama of Buda and the Budai Hills (see **PARKS**, **Budai-hegység**) – benches are at hand! Continue to the north along Tóth Árpád sétány, noticing the Mátyás-templom (see **CHURCHES**, **A-Z**) down Szentháromság utca. Take the next right (Nőegylet utca) and then left into Úri utca (Gentlemen's Street). A stroll along this section of Úri utca is a good introduction to the kind of architecture so typical of the Castle District and so rare elsewhere in the city – fine examples of medieval and baroque town houses, each one sporting individual features. If you look closely you'll notice that all of the buildings have a plaque with *műemlék* on it (equivalent of the blue plaques in London) attesting to their cultural and/or historical importance. Detour to the right halfway along Úri utca and turn left into Országház utca. The old Parliament building which gave the street its name is at No. 28. Wander in and have a look at some of the picturesque courtyards along the street. At the end of the street lies Kapisztrán tér with the Magdolna torony (see **CITY SIGHTS 1**) standing on your left. As you cross over the square towards the castle walls again and the Hadtörténeti Múzeum (see **MUSEUMS 1**, **A-Z**), take a look back down Úri utca which is at its most colourful from this point. The corner of the walls outside the museum is another excellent place from which to view the Buda Hills as well as the activity in Moszkva tér and beyond. Continuing along the walls will take you to the Vienna Gate (Bécsi kapu – see **CITY SIGHTS 1**), another good vantage point. It will also take you behind the large building which houses the National Archives. Coming down off the walls into Bécsi kapu tér – the northernmost square in the district – you will see a neoclassical Lutheran church on the southern side. Walk towards this building and Fortuna utca in order

to pass the Trade and Catering Industrial Museum (see **MUSEUMS 1**, **Kereskedelmi és Vendéglátóipari Múzeum**). Alternatively, you could take the Táncsics Mihály utca to its left. Beethoven spent a very brief period at No. 7 and there is a carefully-preserved medieval Jewish prayer house at No. 26. Both routes lead to Hess András tér and the Hilton Hotel (see **BUILDINGS**, **Budapest Hilton**). The building at No. 3 is known as the Red Hedgehog House and was at one time the only public inn offering lodgings in the city. The square itself is named after the first painter in Buda, who worked at No. 4.

Behind the Hilton and Mátyás Church (see **CHURCHES**, **Mátyás-templom**) is the Fishermen's Bastion (see **CITY SIGHTS 1**, **Halászbástya**). Leave Szentháromság tér (see **A-Z**) along Tárnok utca which will take you past the Arany Sas Patikamúzeum (see **MUSEUMS 1**). Many of the buildings have distinctive medieval features. Some, such as at No. 14, have had the later baroque additions removed to restore the original exteriors. The street used to be very popular with merchants in the Middle Ages as it leads into Dísz tér – the old market place.

The main monument of the square is dedicated to the memory of the soldiers in the 1848-49 War of Independence. Various semi-govern-

mental bodies are housed around the square and the Korona coffee house (see **CAFÉS**) is on the south side. Continuing over the square into Színház utca (Theatre Street) we find, not surprisingly, the Várszínház (Castle Theatre). It was re-opened just over a decade ago after a typical history of destruction and reconstruction. The exterior dimensions do not reflect the more intimate character of the interior. Restoration work on surrounding buildings has not yet been completed and bullet holes which have been there since World War II can still be seen.

Walking onwards across Szent György tér we reach the northern wing of the Király palota (see **BUILDINGS**, **A-Z**) which houses two major museums (see **MUSEUMS 1**). The recently re-opened funicular railway will take you back down the hill to Clark Ádám tér.

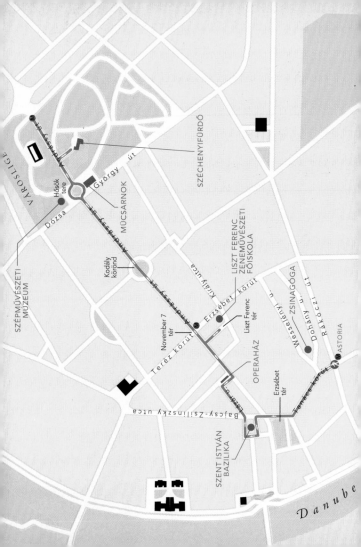

VÁROSLIGET

Széchenyi út

Hősök tere

György út

MŰCSARNOK

SZÉCHENYIFÜRDŐ

Dózsa

Andrássy út

SZÉPMŰVÉSZETI MÚZEUM

Kodály körönd

Andrássy út

Király utca

LISZT FERENC ZENEMŰVÉSZETI FŐISKOLA

Liszt Ferenc tér

Erzsébet körút

ZSINAGÓGA

Wesselényi u.

Dohány u.

Rákóczi út

ASTORIA

Teréz körút

November 7 tér

OPERAHÁZ

Károly körút

Tanács körút

Bajcsy-Zsilinszky utca

Erzsébet tér

SZENT ISTVÁN BAZILIKA

D a n u b e

Approximately 2 hr 30 min.

From the Astoria underground station take Tanács körút northwards. At the point where it meets Wesselényi utca and Dohány utca on the right you will see the Synagogue (see **CHURCHES**, **Zsinagóga**). Continue along Tanács körút towards the former Deák Ferenc tér (see **Erzsébet tér**) and you will pass a Lutheran church. A little further on is Erzsébet tér with the main coach station. Continue along Bajcsy-Zsilinsky utca until you reach Andrássy út on the right. If you have not yet seen the Basilica (see **CHURCHES**, **Szent István bazilika**) now is your chance. It's further along Bajcsy-Zsilinszky utca on the left with the main entrance facing away from the street. Cross the street and take Lázár utca straight ahead which will take you up to the Opera House (see **BUILDINGS**, **Operaház**). Opposite you will see the State Ballet Institute in a French Renaissance-style building designed by Lechner in 1883. Further along Andrássy út you come to Liszt Ferenc tér to the right and Jókai tér on the left. Walk into the former and situated on the left of the junction with Király utca is the Franz Liszt Academy of Music (see **CULTURE**). Take a glimpse into Király utca – King's Street – which used to be one of the most elegant streets of the capital. Retrace your steps to Andrássy út and a few metres further on you will find yourself on November 7 tér at which point the avenue crosses Teréz körút. Taking the Metro here will give you the chance to admire the oldest underground line in continental Europe, completed in 1896. Take Line 1 in the direction of Mexikói út and get off after two stops at Kodály körönd, a circular square named after the famous composer (see **Kodály**). There are four statues in the square including those of Bálint Balassi, an outstanding 16thC poet, and Vak Botthán who was a general in the fight for independence from the Habsburgs in the 18thC. As you continue along the avenue it becomes less closely built up as it gets nearer Hősök tere (see **A-Z**). Situated on the square are two museums, the Szépművészeti Múzeum and the Műcsarnok (see **MUSEUMS 2**). Beyond, a bridge leads over an artificial lake which functions as an ice-rink in winter. This lake is part of the City Park (see **PARKS**, **Városliget**) and the Vajdahunyad vára (see **BUILDINGS**, **A-Z**) offers a fine background to a stroll. Continue into the park along Andrássy út to pass the Széchenyifürdő (see **Thermal Baths**). A Metro stop is situated right in front and this gets you back into town.

Accidents & Breakdowns: Following an accident, it is not obligatory to inform the police if there is no personal injury, less than 15,000 Ft worth of damage, and both parties agree over details. Otherwise the police should be called and everyone should remain at the scene of the accident until they arrive. For insurance claims, foreigners must report an accident, within 24 hours, to Hungaria Biztosító, Budapest V, Aranykéz u. 2, tel: 1183016. You will need proof of insurance, a receipt for any medical expenses and a report of injuries. Assistance in cases of breakdown is provided by the 'Yellow Angels' of the MAK (Magyar Autóklub). As soon as you arrive in Hungary you should obtain a free Breakdown Card at the border crossing point or at any MAK office (see **Driving**). In the event of a breakdown, give it to a passing motorist who will hand it in at the nearest service point (in theory, at least). On the motorways the system is more conventional and there are emergency phones with direct link-up to MAK. If you break down in Budapest tel: 1691831/1693714 (24 hr). The service is free to members of affiliated clubs. Spare parts for foreign cars, when they can be found, are often very expensive. See **Emergency Numbers**.

Accommodation: Whilst tourist accommodation is plentiful in Budapest, it is always advisable to book your room well in advance – in summer because it is the busiest tourist season and in winter because Budapest is a popular exhibition and conference centre. However, if you do arrive without a room the tourist offices should be able to find you one somewhere (see **Tourist Information**). You can expect an out-of-season discount (about 30%). Hotels are graded according to the international star system of five stars for luxury accommodation to one star for the basics. Most hotels from three to five stars have their own boutiques and organize sightseeing tours, etc. Inns, or pensions, offer more intimate and homely accommodation for both individuals and small groups. They are divided into two categories – first and second class – and prices in Budapest are not much cheaper than their hotel equivalent. They do not usually have the 24-hr desk service provided by hotels. There are also several self-contained holiday flats and 'tourist accommodations' which have five or more beds to a room. See **Camping & Caravanning**, **Youth Hostels**.

Airport: Budapest airport is situated 16 km southeast of the city at
Ferihegy. There is no internal air network in Hungary, so both terminals
are international – Terminal 1 (tel: 1572122) serves foreign air companies and Terminal 2 (tel: 1579123) MALÉV flights. Amenities include a
bureau de change, a tax-free shop, taxi and rent-a-car agencies (see
Car Hire), post office, bar/restaurant, newspaper stand and accommodation service. The bus link to Budapest (Erzsébet tér) is by the VOLÁN
bus (see **Buses**), which operates from 0500-2300 every half hour and
takes 40 min (25 Ft to Terminal 1 and 35 Ft to Terminal 2). From
Terminal 1 they leave at 10 and 40 min past the hour and from Erzsébet
tér on the hour and half past the hour. Bus 193 acts as a shuttle
between the airport and the terminus of Metro line 3. A taxi to the city
centre will cost you about 400 Ft.

Andrássy út: Perhaps the most beautiful avenue in Budapest, 2.5
km long. There are many architectural treats, from the Opera House at
No. 22 (see **BUILDINGS**, **Operaház**) to the fine buildings surrounding the
Kodály körönd. The former Academy of Music is at No. 67 and the
Academy of Fine Arts is at No. 71. The avenue has had several names
since it was completed in 1876. At one point Joseph Stalin was incorporated into the title but this was changed to something less provoca-
tive following the 1956 uprising. Only recently its name has been
changed from Népköztársaság útja, reverting to its older name of
Andrássy ut. See **WALK 3**.

Aquincum: Situated north of the present-day district of Óbuda,
Aquincum was the capital of the Roman province of Lower Pannonia
and was founded in the 1stC AD. Excavations have revealed a settlement equipped with a sewage system, public baths and sports facilities. It is thought that the town accommodated the civilians who provided
the Roman army with support services. See **CITY SIGHTS 2**, **MUSEUMS 1**.

Baby-sitters: As there are no organized baby-sitting services in
Budapest, it is best to make enquiries at your hotel reception.

Banks: See Money, Opening Times.

Aquincum

Bartók, Béla (1881-1945):
One of the best-known of
Hungarian musicians, Bartók was
greatly interested in Hungarian
folklore and spent much of his
time and energy in recording folk
songs. He later incorporated folk
music into his own compositions
for piano, orchestra and violin. He
was also greatly inspired by
Debussy and Stravinsky and his
most important works are
undoubtedly his string quartets.
His music is very personal but
accessible, which accounts for its
popularity. A museum dedicated
to Bartók is in Óbuda, at Csalán u.
29, in a building where the composer used to live. Open 1000-
1800 Tue.-Sun.

**Belvárosi Plébánia-tem-
plom:** The baroque exterior of
this church disguises parts which
date from the 12thC building
which, in turn, was constructed
using stones from the old Roman
walls. As such the church consti-
tutes the oldest building in
Budapest. It was used as a mosque
during the Turkish occupation and
evidence of this is seen in its interior. Imre Steindl was responsible
for one of the many periods of
restoration the church has undergone. See **CHURCHES**.

Best Buys: Craftwork from all over Hungary can be seen in the Intertourist, Konsumtourist, Utastourist and Panuouia shops in the city centre, hotel foyers and airport (see **A-Z**). Perhaps the best-known of Hungarian crafts is Herend porcelain. Leather is good value, either in the form of gloves, shoes and coats or articles created for the tourist market. You will find embroidery and lace-work everywhere and a delicately-sewn tablecloth, a peasant's blouse or a set of handkerchiefs make ideal presents if you are worried about excess lug-gage fees. Sculpted wood-work is plentiful – a chess set, for example, makes a fine souvenir. Classical and folk music tapes and records are ideal for recapturing the atmosphere of your holiday. There are also inexpensive oriental rugs and carpets for sale. On the culinary side, paprika and other spices are always a good buy as well as salami. A bottle of *Tokaji* (see **Drinks**) is guaranteed to evoke happy memories back home. See **SHOPPING**, **Shopping**.

Bicycle & Motorbike Hire: There are no bicycle or motorbike hire facilities in Budapest. The closest you get is on Margaret Island (see **PARKS**, **Margitsziget**) at 'Bringo Hintó', which hires out pedal-propelled carriages and go-karts to visit the island at 100 Ft per hr.

Budai-hegység: A hilly region to the west and northwest of Budapest. The region offers city dwellers and tourists alike the chance to enjoy the fresh air and the forest walks along the gentle slopes. As well as by road, the hills can be reached and explored by taking the cog-wheel railway from Városmajor (see **PARKS**) to Széchenyi-hegy (Liberty Hill). Near the top terminus you will find the Pioneer Railway (see **CHILDREN**). The Libegő (chair lift) will convey you from Zugligeti út to the vantage point at the top of Jánoshegy, where there is a 23 m-high lookout tower designed by the architect of the Fishermen's Bastion (see **CITY SIGHTS 1, Halászbástya**). Most of the footpaths are clearly marked with some indication of time and distance. Some of these routes have been turned into nature trails – the wildlife and vegetation is surprisingly abundant considering the proximity to the city. See **PARKS**.

Budapest Hilton: Béla Pintér was the architect of this building which, after initial controversy, has attracted more praise than criticism since its completion in 1976. By incorporating the remains of a Dominican church and a Jesuit monastery and by the use of reflective glass, it manages to impose its own character without looking out of place in its surroundings. See **BUILDINGS, WALK 2**.

Budapesti Történeti Múzeum: The Historical Museum, but often called the Vármúzeum (Castle Museum). The exhibition on the main floor is entitled *Two Thousand Years of Budapest* and outlines the history of the city from Roman times, through to the Turkish occupation and the age of the Magyars. However, the museum principally focuses on the reconstruction of the Királyi palota (see **BUILDINGS, A-Z**). Several rooms have undergone varying degrees of restoration. Most of the artefacts on display were found during excavation work on Castle Hill and many of the murals and statues are similarly authentic. The marble reliefs in the Great Gothic Hall are impressive. See **MUSEUMS 1**.

Budget:	Hotel breakfast	from 150 Ft
	Dish of the day	from 250 Ft
	Dinner	from 800 Ft
	Beer/Lager	60-120 Ft
	Wine (shop)	from 80 Ft per bottle
	Wine (restaurant)	from 200 Ft per bottle
	Fruit Juice	60-70 Ft per litre
	Coffee and Pastries	from 30 Ft
	Museum Ticket	from 10 Ft

Buses: In Budapest you are never far from a bus stop (rectangular boards carrying the outline of a bus and the initial 'M'). Most services operate from 0430-2300 though numbers 3, 42, 78, 111, 144, 173, 179 and 182 offer a night service as do buses marked with a 'C' (from the Western Railway Station to Margaret Island). Buses with red numbers on them are fast services, those with an 'A' are limited stop and those marked with an 'E' only stop at the two terminals. The free city map from Tourinform (see **Tourist Information**) indicates the main bus routes and there is also a route map at most stops. Before boarding, you must have one of the blue bus tickets which cost 10 Ft (you will need 5 x 2 Ft coins for the machines). Alternatively, you can buy a 24-hr ticket, valid on the day you buy it, which can be used for unlimited travel on bus, tram, trolleybus and underground within the city limits (80 Ft). To validate the ticket, punch it into one of the red machines by the doors and when you want to get off press the green light button above the door. Coaches: The VOLÁN Company provides a regular service between Budapest and Vienna, Salzburg, Graz, Klagenfurt, Semmering, Munich and Venice from the International Coach Station at Erzsébet tér (tel: 1172511/1172369). The amenities at the station include a café, a left-luggage office, reservations desks and toilets. See **Transport**.

Cameras & Photography: Flash photography is allowed in museums and churches unless otherwise indicated. Film is relatively cheap and readily available, although it is best to bring your own supply of slide films. Kodak operates through a company called Fotex and you will see their modern developing labs dotted around the city.

Camping & Caravanning: Camp sites in Hungary are graded from one to four stars (luxury) depending on hygienic installations and amenities offered. Most of those in the Budapest area are three-star establishments and open from May to September. There are about six to choose from, though it should be noted that the Lake Balaton region (see **EXCURSION 2**) is a much more popular camping area for obvious reasons. For a complete list of camp sites apply to the Magyar Camping és Caravanning Club at Budapest VIII, Üllői út 6, tel: 1336536. Some sites offer reductions to members of the International Camping and Caravanning Club (FICC). You will be charged per unit (80-100 Ft) and per person (25-50 Ft) plus a parking fee and fee for use of electric connection. Children from 2-14 only pay half price and considerable reductions are offered out of season. See **Accommodation**.

Car Hire: Avis, Hertz, Europcar and Budget all work in association with various Hungarian travel agencies and have offices in Budapest: Avis-Ibusz: V, Martinelli tér 8, tel: 1186222; Europcar-Volántourist: IX, Vaskapu u. 16, tel: 1334783; Budget-Cooptourist: I, Mészáros u. 56/a, tel: 1752058; Hertz-Főtaxi: VII, Kertész u. 24, tel: 1116116. They also have offices at the airport (see **A-Z**). The conditions for hiring a car are similar to those in other countries – you must be 21 or over and have held a licence for at least a year. Credit cards are welcome as a form of payment which dispenses with the need for a deposit (otherwise expect to pay a deposit of about US $150). See **Driving**.

Castle of Vajdahunyad: See **Vajdahunyad vára**.

Chemists: Chemists (*gyógyszertár*) in Budapest deal exclusively in drugs and herbs and do not sell cosmetic products of any kind. Some shops are worth entering just to see the display of bottles and jars (the Pázmány Péter Patika on Egyetem tér and the Kígyó Patika in Kossuth Lajos u. 2/a, both in the 5th district). Jugs of water and glasses are provided so you can take your medicine on the spot. Many chemists speak German and English. Closing time for most is 2000 but you will find the address of the nearest open pharmacy in the window. The following provide a permanent night service: Frankel Leó u. 22; Rákóczi u. 86;

Kosztolányi Dezső tér 11; Alkotás u. 1/b; Bosnyák u. 1/a. Ring the night bell and the chemist will serve you through a small window.

Children: There are numerous parks and playgrounds all over Budapest where you can have picnics and let the children run around (see **PARKS**). The museums, buildings and monuments may not always hold much interest for them, but there are other activities more tailored to their needs (see **CHILDREN**). Most baby products are obtainable in the department stores and bigger supermarkets but articles like nappies, for example, are relatively expensive.

Citadella: A fortress on Gellért Hill (see PARKS, **Gellérthegy**), built in the mid-19thC and now used as a hotel, restaurant, museum and night-club. The Germans retreated here in a desperate last attempt to resist the Soviet advance during World War II and the building was badly damaged. The southeast corner of the fortifications affords a magnificent view of the whole city. See BUILDINGS.

City Hall: See BUILDINGS, **Fővárosi Tanács**.

City Park: See PARKS, **Városliget**.

View North from Gellérthegy

Climate: Budapest, like the rest of Hungary, enjoys a moderate climate with the coldest month being January (average temperature 1°C) and the hottest July (average temperature 22°C). Rainfall is not excessive with about 2000 hours of sunshine per year.

Complaints: If you have been overcharged, or find that prices do not correspond to those displayed, ask to see the owner or manager of the premises and try to sort out any misunderstanding.

Consulates:
UK – V, Harmincad u. 6, tel: 1182828.
Australia – VI, Délibáb u. 30, tel: 1534233.
Canada – II, Budakeszi út 32, tel: 1767711.
USA – V, Szabadság tér 12, tel: 1126450.

Conversion Chart:

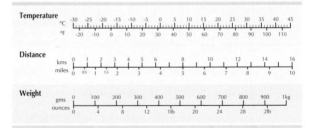

Credit Cards: See Money.

Crime & Theft: The usual precautions should be taken in order not to tempt the would-be thief. Do not leave valuables on display in parked cars or carry wallets sticking out of back pockets. In general the crime rate is low in Hungary, but watch out for pickpockets, especially in crowded shopping streets. It is also advisable to steer clear of anybody offering to change money for you at black-market rates. If you are the victim of a crime, contact the police immediately. They will provide you with the necessary documents for any insurance claim. See **Emergency Numbers**, **Insurance**, **Police**.

Currency: The Hungarian monetary unit is the Forint (Ft) which contains 100 fillers (f). There are 10, 20 and 50 filler and 1, 2, 5 and 10 Forint coins. Banknotes come in denominations of 10, 20, 50, 100, 500 and 1000 Ft. For local phone calls and public transport ticket machines you will need an endless supply of 2 and 5 Ft coins. See **Money**.

Customs & Behaviour: Physical contact is important to the Hungarians and you will often see people hugging, shaking hands and kissing each other on the cheeks. Not many local people speak English but the older generation speaks German.

Customs Allowances:

Duty Free Into:	Cigarettes	*or* Cigars	*or* Tobacco	Spirits	Wine
HG	250	50	250 g	1 *l*	2 *l*
UK	200	50	250 g	1 *l*	2 *l*

Danube: See **Duna**.

Deák Ferenc tér: See **Erzsébet tér**.

Dentists: See **Health**.

Disabled People: There are very few facilities for the handicapped, and transport and access to buildings is often difficult. Most of the bigger hotels cater for guests in wheelchairs but accommodation in private homes or inns is practically out of the question. Hopefully, this aspect of tourism in Budapest will be developed in the near future.

Doctors: See **Health**.

Drinks: The sunny climate and long, warm autumn make wine growing important in Hungary and the local wines are well worth sampling. The most famous one is *Tokaji* which is either *furmint* (dry), *szamorodni* (medium) or *aszu* (sweet). The degree of sweetness and quality is indicated by a number on the label. Other white wines include the popular *Badacsonyi kéknyelű*, *Egerszóláti olaszrizling* and many made from Hungarian-grown French grapes such as Chardonnay and Sauvignon. They tend to be light and fruity, similar to a German riesling, and will have either the word *édes* (sweet) or *száraz* (dry) on the label. Among the red wines, try the *Pinot Noir* (from Pécs), the full-bodied *Villányi Burgundi* and the heavy *Egri Bikavér* (Eger bull's blood). Whilst Hungarians mostly prefer imported beers you might enjoy Budapest's own *Dreher Pils* which is a lot less gassy. Czech and East German brands are also good. Draught beer is rare and not recommended. All the familiar brands of soft drinks are made in Hungary under licence and are much better than local imitations. 'Pure' fruit juice usually has sugar added to it. Mineral water is good and cheap – ask for *asvány víz* – but watch out for the sulphurous ones! Finally, the coffee is usually of the 'espresso' type, but in better cafés there is often a greater choice.

Driving: In order to bring your car into Hungary, you will need an international insurance policy, the car's registration document and a valid driving licence as well as your passport and visa. If you do not have international insurance you are required to pay a car insurance tax at the border which only covers damage caused to Hungarian citizens. In addition, you are supposed to carry a first-aid kit, a warning triangle, a nationality sticker and spare bulbs for the car lights. Seat belts are compulsory in the front and children under six must travel in the back. Horns should not be used unless it is absolutely essential and dipped headlights must be on from dusk to dawn. Driving after having had a drink is strictly illegal and it is advisable not to drive if you have taken any form of sedative. Random breath tests are carried out. The speed limits are 120 kph on motorways, 80 kph on highways and 60 kph in built up areas. Priority is to the right although on roundabouts priority is to those already in motion. Any violation of these regulations can mean a fairly hefty on-the-spot fine of 500-1000 Ft. It is best not to dispute the decision of the police as this can lead to lengthy and usually fruitless proceedings. Petrol is readily available throughout Hungary at 30-35 Ft per litre and lead-free petrol is becoming more common. Diesel oil can only be bought using tickets purchased from IBUSZ offices (see **Tourist Information**) and border crossing points. These are not refundable. Most petrol stations are open 0600-2200, and there should be no problem in finding a 24-hr service in Budapest or on main roads. The Magyar Autóklub (MAK) offers reciprocal membership to affiliated touring clubs such the AA. Their office is at Rómer Flóris u. 4, tel: 1152040. They also offer a foreign-language information service, tel: 1353101. As driving is restricted in most of the 5th district of the city and parking is not easy anywhere, it is best to use public transport. On the edge of the Inner City zone there are four parking areas – Martinelli tér, Erzsébet tér, Március 15 tér and Belgrád rakpart as well as the free car parks at every Metro terminus. Driving in the Castle District is only allowed for those with a special permit and guests at the Hilton! See **Accidents & Breakdowns**.

Drugs: Narcotics are strictly illegal and any abuse is punished.

Duna: One of Europe's greatest rivers, the Danube flows from the west to the south through all of Hungary as well as Budapest itself. It forms a major line of communication with cities such as Vienna. Within Budapest, the river can be admired from one of the many bridges linking Buda with Pest. Boat trips to the towns along the Danube Bend (see EXCURSION 1) can be booked at the Vigadó tér terminal.

Eating Out: Within the last few years a large number of restaurants has sprung up all over Budapest. As is to be expected with such a rapid development, many don't last long, but some are earning a reputation for good quality. It is still relatively cheap to eat out well in Budapest. There is no single area with a concentration of restaurants and many of them are not easy to get to. The cheaper Hungarian-style restaurants do not usually have anything marked up in English so ordering may be tricky. Desserts are often on the first page of the restaurant menu and drinks on a completely different menu. You will often have to rely on the waiter's choice of wine. As a rough guide, dinner will cost upwards of 1000 Ft in an expensive restaurant, between 500 and 1000 Ft in a moderately-priced one, and under 500 Ft in an inexpensive establishment. See **RESTAURANTS**.

Eger: 132 km east of Budapest. Pop: 60,000. Motorway 3, then Roads 3 and 25; bus from Erzsébet tér; train from Keleti pályaudvar. A town famous for its wine, formerly for its thermal baths, and for its resistance to the Turkish invasion. The town's most rapid development took place during the 18thC, hence the dominance of baroque architecture. The mid-19thC cathedral is the second-largest religious building in Hungary after the Basilica in Esztergom (see **EXCURSION 1**, **A-Z**). The teachers' training college is the country's largest baroque building; other noteworthy examples of this style include the County Hall in Kossuth Lajos utca with its fine wrought-iron gate. The 14-sided minaret at the end of Knézich Károly utca is Europe's northernmost minaret, dating from the period of the Turkish invasion.

Egyetemi templom: This beautiful baroque church dates from 1725-42 and was built by András Mayeshoffer for the monks of the Order of St. Paul (the only monastic order of Hungarian origin). The bulb-shaped spires and towers were completed in 1768 and 1781. The sculptured gate and elaborate ornamental carvings are the work of the monks themselves. The statues on the high altar are attributed to József Habenstrit. Note also the interesting pulpit and organ. See **CHURCHES**.

Electricity: The electric current is 220 V and 50 C throughout the country and the plugs are of the Continental two-pin variety. An adaptor is needed for UK appliances.

Emergency Numbers:

Police	07
Ambulance	04
Fire	05

See **Accidents & Breakdowns**, **Health**, **Police**.

Erzsébet tér: Formerly called Engels tér, this square forms the nucleus of Pest's commercial area. The adjoining area, once the location of Deák Ferenc tér, is now a construction site. The park in Erzsébet tér contains an interesting fountain designed by Miklós Ybl and statues originally designed by Leó Feszler and Béla Brestyánszky though Dezső Győri had to remodel them in 1959 as they had been damaged during the war. The British Embassy lies in the small street linking Erzsébet tér and Vörösmarty tér.

Esztergom: 46 km northwest of Budapest. Pop: 28,000. Road 11; Roads 10 and 111; bus from Erzsébet tér; train from Nyugati pályaudvar; passenger boat from Vigadó tér. An important town since Roman times and capital of Hungary in the 10thC, it is the seat of the archbishopric of Esztergom. After prospering in the 12thC, it was destroyed by the Turks. The Basilica, the largest church in the country, dates from 1822-60. It houses a magnificent Treasury which boasts a golden Calvary cross of King Matthias and other religious artefacts. The south side of the cathedral incorporates stones from part of the original church. Nearby is a rebuilt section of the royal medieval palace, and the Christian Museum, which contains a fine collection of 18thC paintings, with particular emphasis on German, Austrian and Italian artists. A stroll along the Kis Duna (small Danube) is a pleasant way to return to the town centre but you should also wander through the back streets to fully appreciate the provincial style. See **EXCURSION 1**.

Events:

February: The Budapest Film Festival (*Filmszemle*).

15 March: National Day, when people commemorate the 1848 revolution; *late March:* The Spring Festival, Hungarian and international artists, music, fine arts, theatre, folklore. The festival's central office is at Vörösmarty tér 1.

1 May: May Day procession, arts and crafts fair, concerts and performances all day in Városliget (see **PARKS**, **A-Z**) and Tabán Park; *Friday nearest 20 May:* opening of the Budapest International Fair (BNV); *last week of May:* Book Fair.

August: Open-air concerts, theatrical performances; *20:* St. Stephen's Day, parades on the Danube, fly-pasts, firework display; *Late August:* Formula 1 Grand Prix at Mogyoród.

September: The Budapest Autumn International Fair, displays of consumer goods; *25:* Budapest Arts Week, Bartók's birthday (see **Bartók**), music, dance and drama performances, art exhibitions.

Ferenc József (1830-1916): Generally known outside Hungary as Franz Joseph, he was officially crowned emperor of Austria in 1848 due to the illness of his uncle, Ferdinand I (1835-48). However, he was already ruling the country, along with his popular wife Elizabeth, at the time of the unsuccessful War of Independence (1848-49) fought by Hungary against Austrian rule.

Ferencesek Temploma: Built in 1727-43 in baroque style on the site of a 13thC church and used as a mosque by the Turks. The neo-Gothic spire was completed in 1863. Set into the church wall on the Kossuth Lajos utca side is a relief by Barnabás Holló called *The Flood Mariner* (1905). It honours the heroism of Baron Miklós Wesselényi, who saved many lives during the 1838 flood. See **CHURCHES, WALK 1**.

Fishermen's Bastion: See Halászbástya.

Food: Hungarian cuisine is rather heavy, with a lot of animal fat used for cooking and plenty of sauces made from sour cream. Paprika is used in numerous dishes but usually subtly blended with other spices. Soups are excellent either as a main course at lunch time or as a starter for dinner. Traditional Hungarian Gulasch (*gulyás*) is a meat (or fish) and potato soup and not stew (which the Hungarians call *pörkölt*). Pancakes are also a popular starter and, accompanied by a bowl of soup, once represented the staple diet for Hungarian families. Try the *hortobágyi húsos palacsinta* (pancakes stuffed with meat, spices and cream). Favourite meats are pork and veal and goose liver is considered to be a speciality. You will see some recurrent terms on a menu such as Hungarian-style (with onion, paprika and sour cream sauce) and Viennese-style. Carp and trout are popular fish as is *fogas*

– a fish from Lake Balaton. Vegetables vary in both availability and price according to season and are usually very tasty. Stuffed cabbage and peppers are worth a try. Salads are plentiful and a good way to counterbalance the richness of the main course – try the refreshing cucumber salad. If you can face dessert after all that you will find that sour cream still features, this time accompanying pancakes and strudels of various fillings with a sprinkling of nuts, cinnamon and dried fruit replacing the paprika. Try *túró gombóc* – cheese balls served hot with cream and cinnamon. Fresh fruits are served in season.

Fő tér: Formerly the most important square in the Óbuda district. Noteworthy buildings include the former Zichy Mansion on the east side, but others have been renovated to a very high standard as well. Although the square has been pedestrianized, the visitor must still watch out for horse-drawn carriages.

Fővárosi Tanács: The City Hall, the largest baroque building in the city, was designed by Anton Martinelli and completed in 1735. After periods as a barracks and a home for disabled soldiers, it has been used as the City Hall since 1894. See BUILDINGS.

Franz Joseph: See Ferenc József.

Gellért, Szent (c.980-1046): A Venetian priest called to Hungary to educate St. Stephen's son, Imre (see **István**). He helped in converting the people to Christianity and was martyred in 1046 on the hill now known as Gellérthegy (see **A-Z**).

Gellérthegy: Halfway up this hill, facing Erzsébet-híd (Elizabeth Bridge), is a monument to Szent Gellért (see CITY SIGHTS 1, **Gellért**) and a waterfall that is lit up at night. At the top of the hill lie the Citadella (see BUILDINGS, **A-Z**) and the Liberation Monument (see CITY SIGHTS 1). On the southern and western slopes sprawls Jubilee Park, completed in 1965/66. The view of the Budai-hegység (see PARKS, **A-Z**) is magnificent. There is a relief entitled *Budapest* by István Kiss in the park and also *St. Gellért's Fountain* by Ferenc Medgyessy. See PARKS.

Guides: See Tourist Information.

Hadtörténeti Múzeum: Housed in a former barracks, the Military Museum contains weaponry ranging from medieval times to the present day. Also on display are maps, documents, paintings and woodcuts relating to local military history. Special attention is given to the battles of the last two centuries, including the 1848-49 War of Independence and the devastating period at the end of World War II. See MUSEUMS 1.

Halászbástya: A neo-Romanesque/neo-Gothic facade constructed between 1901 and 1903 to the design of Frigyes Schulek. The name derives from its location, the site of a former fish market. There are marvellous views over the Danube (see **Duna**) and Transylvanian embroidery is sold on the terraces. See CITY SIGHTS 1, WALK 2.

Health: All first-aid treatment in hospitals and clinics is free though you will have to pay if you need to consult a doctor or a dentist. For this reason, health insurance is highly recommended. Ask at the hotel reception or your consulate (see **A-Z**) for an English-speaking doctor or dentist. There is a 24-hr dental service at Budapest VIII, Mária u. 52, tel: 1330189. Budapest is an extremely healthy place to be, with the thermal baths (see **A-Z**) serving as a magic cure for a wide range of ailments. See **Chemists, Emergency Numbers, Insurance**.

Hopp Ferenc Múzeum: This museum is named after the man who left his personal collection of Japanese and Indian artefacts to the nation, and also his villa to house it in. Asian items from various other collections have been added since his death. See MUSEUMS 2.

Hősök tere: Heroes' Square, the focal point of which is the Millennial Memorial (see CITY SIGHTS 1, **Millenniumi Emlékmű**), flanked by the Szépművészeti Múzeum (1916 – see MUSEUMS 2) and the Műcsarnok (1895), an art gallery. The former is neoclassical with a Corinthian facade, and the latter resembles a Greek temple. Both buildings were designed by Albert Schickedanz and Fülöp Herzog.

Iparművészeti Múzeum

Hospitals: See **Health**.

Hungarian National Gallery: See MUSEUMS 1, **Magyar Nemzeti Galéria**.

Hunting & Fishing: The Hungarian Enterprise for Game Trading (MAVAD) office is at Úri u. 39, tel: 1759611. Apply to them for a hunting permit. Hunting seasons are: deer, Sep.-Jan.; roebuck, May-Sep.; fallow buck and moufflon, Oct.-Jan.; wild boar, all year; pheasant, Oct.-Feb.; hare, Oct.-Dec.; wild duck, Aug.-Jan.

The Fishing Association office is at Bem József u. 4. Open 0800-1700 weekdays only. Permits are issued on receipt of a passport. The cost depends on the area – Lake Balaton is 150 Ft per day, 550 Ft per week; Lake Velence is 120 Ft per day, 450 Ft per week. Catfish, pike, bream, carp, and perch are available. Fishing is forbidden on Lake Balaton between 20 April and the end of May.

Inner City Parish Church: See **Belvárosi Plébánia-templom**.

Insurance: You are recommended to take out travel insurance before your trip. Your travel agent should be able to advise you on the most suitable policy. See **Crime & Theft**, **Driving**, **Health**.

Iparművészeti Múzeum: This magnificent building is the home of the Museum of Applied Arts. It is unique, with an interesting blend of Arabic, Hindu and Hungarian folk motifs. The museum is perhaps better known for its temporary exhibitions from other countries, but it also has a large collection of ceramics, textiles, metalwork and furniture made by Hungarian craftsmen and women through the ages. Works from other European countries are also on display, and there is also a Chinese section. See MUSEUMS 2.

István, Szent (c.975-1038): Stephen belonged to the Árpád dynasty, was crowned King of Hungary (Stephen I) in 1000 and in 1083 was made a saint. A ruthless and intelligent man, he enforced the feudal system and introduced Christianity to his country. He ordered the building of churches and the working of the land – unpopular measures with the nomadic population but changes that ended their wandering-thieving way of life.

Kecskemét: 85 km southeast of Budapest. Pop: 100,000. Road 5; train from Keleti pályaudvar. Important as the agricultural centre of the Great Plain. Kossuth Lajos tér has a wonderful Town Hall built in the style that became known as New Hungarian. It boasts a magnificent ceremonial hall with an impressive chandelier. In front is a stone marking the spot where the dramatist József Katona died of a heart attack in 1830 and the square nearby contains the Katona József Theatre. Three churches share the square with the Town Hall – a Calvinist, Catholic and former Franciscan Church. Szabadság tér has a former synagogue (recently restored) and the Art Nouveau Cifra Palace to its credit. Zoltán Kodály (see **A-Z**) is a famous son of the town and has a music academy named after him. See **EXCURSION 4**.

Kereskedelmi és Vendéglátóipari Múzeum: The Trade and Catering Industrial Museum, which shows the history of catering in Hungary from Roman times. However, most of the exhibits are related to the last couple of centuries with the interior of a *csárda* (inn) and an old Buda confectioner's among the more interesting set-pieces. The Trade section concentrates more on business and depicts the development of trade in Hungary in recent times. See **MUSEUMS 1**.

Keszthely: 192 km west of Budapest. Road 71; train from Déli pályaudvar. A pretty town situated on the northwest side of Lake Balaton, with some fine baroque buildings. The imposing Festetics Palace in Kossuth Lajos utca contains the Helikon Library and a ballroom sometimes used for chamber music recitals. Also of interest are the surrounding buildings and a Balaton museum. The Catholic church in Fő tér dates from the 14thC. See **EXCURSION 2**.

Kina Múzeum: Housed in a villa, this museum is devoted to Chinese art and its collection of ceramics and sculpture is particularly noteworthy. See **MUSEUMS 2**.

Királyi palota: The history of the Royal Palace is as turbulent as that of the whole country. The original castle was built in the 13thC and it became an integral part of the city's commercial, cultural and intellectual life in medieval times, especially during the 15thC. The Turkish occupation saw a decline in importance and state of repair, with further damage being inflicted during the later battles to defeat the Turks (it was, in fact, more or less destroyed in 1686). The 1848-49 War of Independence and then World War II brought more destruction and reconstruction. It now houses the Széchenyi Library as well as the Hungarian National Gallery (see **MUSEUMS 1**, **Magyar Nemzeti Galéria**) and the Budapest Museum of History (**MUSEUMS 1**, **Budapesti Történeti Múzeum**). See **BUILDINGS**.

Kiskörút: The 'Little Boulevard', which marks the limits of the Inner City Area, follows the path of the old city wall near Erzsébet tér (see **A-Z**) to Liberty Bridge. It incorporates Tanács körút, Múzeum körút and Tolbuhin körút. Unlike the Nagykörút (see **A-Z**), many fine buildings can be found along this boulevard – including the Central Market Hall (see **Markets**), Nemzeti Múzeum (see **MUSEUMS 2**, **A-Z**), Karl Marx University and Deák Ferenc tér Evangelical Church.

Kodály, Zoltán (1882-1967): A composer who worked with Bartók (see **A-Z**), collecting folk tunes in order to preserve them for future generations and incorporating this ethnic music into his choral works. In addition, he developed a sign system to identify notes without having to read sheet music, a system which is widely used in teaching music to children in the USA and Japan.

Laundries: Privately-owned laundromats and laundries are on the increase and you can either do your washing yourself or leave it and pick it up the next day. Look out for the *Patyolat* chain. There are laundries at: Fő u. 10; József Nádor tér 9; Liszt Ferenc tér 9; József krt. 44.

Liberation Monument: See CITY SIGHTS 1, Szabadság Szobor.

Liszt, Ferenc (1811-86): Liszt developed from a child prodigy into Hungary's foremost composer and he is considered to be a master of harmony. His most notable works include the *Faust Symphony* and the *Dante Symphony*. Although he lived mostly abroad, he was proud of his Hungarian nationality and played an important part in establishing the teaching of music in Hungary. A permanent commemorative exhibition is on display in his former house at Vörösmarty u. 24, open 1200-1800 Mon.-Fri., 1000-1700 Sat. Entry is 5 Ft. Performances of his work are also held here as it contains concert and rehearsal rooms used by the Ferenc Liszt Academy of Music (see CULTURE, WALK 3).

Lost Property: The central lost property office is at Erzsébet tér 5, tel: 1174961. For all objects lost on public transport within Budapest apply to BKV, Akácfa u. 18, tel: 1226613. 0730-1500 Mon., Tue., Thu., Fri.; 0730-1900 Wed. If you leave anything in a taxi contact the company concerned (see **Taxis**).

Magyar Nemzeti Galéria: The permanent exhibition of this gallery includes Hungarian painting and sculpture dating from medieval times to the 20thC as well as Roman and Gothic sculpture. Particular attention is given to baroque art and the romantic painters of the last century – such as Munkácsy and Csontváry. The collection of the late-Gothic winged altar pieces is noteworthy. A selection from the graphic art collection is permanently on display but most contemporary art is usually shown in temporary exhibitions. Chamber and choral music performances take place in the central hall. See MUSEUMS 1.

Margitsziget: An elite residential area during the Roman times and well known for its therapeutic springs, this island (2.5 km long, 0.5 km wide) is a popular recreation area with hotels and sporting facilities. Near the southern end of the island is the Centenary Monument which was built in 1972 by István Kiss to commemorate the 100th anniversary of the union of Pest and Buda. Next to the Palatinus Outdoor Baths (which can hold up to 20,000 people) is the city's most exquisite rose garden. There is a turn-of-the-century water tower nearby. The most significant monument on the island is the convent of the Dominican nuns (see **CITY SIGHTS 2**), built by King Béla IV for his daughter Margaret who came to live here in 1251. She was later canonized and the island was named after her. A plaque in the nave of the church ruins marks her burial place. To the north of the monument is the Premonstratensian chapel (see **CHURCHES**, **Premontrei templom**) surrounded by statues of famous Hungarian literary and artistic figures. Another archaeological site on the island is the ruins of the 13th-14thC Franciscan church and monastery and you can also admire the Ramada Grand Hotel and the Thermal Hotel. See **PARKS**.

Markets: The Central Market Hall in Tolbuhin körút, at the end of Váci utca, is a remarkable turn-of-the-century structure and well worth a visit. You will see beautiful displays of dried red paprika, strings of pale green capsicum and garlic galore. Open 0900-1700 Mon.; 0600-1800 Tue.-Thu., Sat.; 0600-1900 Fri. Other markets include the flea market which is open 0800-1800 Mon.-Fri., 0800-1500 Sat. and is in District XIX at Nagykőrösi u. 156. There are also markets at Bosnyák tér (XIV) and Élmunkás tér (XIII, open on Sun.).

Mátyás-templom: Also known as the Church of the Blessed Virgin of Buda, the Matthias Church was originally constructed between 1250 and 1270. Essential reconstruction work (legend has it that the south tower collapsed) during the reign of King Matthias resulted in the introduction of its better-known title. Both his weddings took place here and the building was also the site of the coronation of Franz Joseph (see **Ferenc József**). Liszt (see **A-Z**) composed his *Coronation Mass* for that occasion. Between 1874 and 1896 the building was 'restored' under the supervision of Frigyes Schulek. In reality it was more of a reconstruction as the 18thC sections were largely removed and the stone steeple added along with an exterior based on the original Gothic sections found during excavation work. Restoration work following damage inflicted in 1945 has preserved his interpretation. See **CHURCHES**.

Millenniumi emlékmű: Construction of this monument in Hősök tere (see **A–Z**) began in 1897 – the intention being to commemorate the thousandth anniversary of the conquest of the country – but was only finished in 1929. The central feature is a column with the Archangel Gabriel on top. On the pedestal are statues of Prince Árpád and the leaders of the seven Magyar tribes and behind them are two rows of statues of prominent kings from Hungarian history. Beneath each one is a relief placing the person in his historical context. Above are statues depicting War and Peace, Science and Art. See **CITY SIGHTS 1**.

Money: Foreign currency and traveller's cheques can only be exchanged for Forints at official exchange points which include the National Bank of Hungary, branch offices of the National Savings Bank (OTP), all commercial banks, travel agencies, tourist offices, hotel companies, appointed hotels and camp sites. You will need your passport for all transactions. Always keep your exchange slip which you will need to show if you want to exchange money back on leaving the country. If you lose a cheque or cheque book contact the National Bank of Hungary at Budapest V, Szabadság tér 8/9, tel: 1532600, 0830-1130 Mon.-Fri. Credit cards are widely accepted in hotels, restaurants, car-hire agencies and department stores. Traveller's cheques and Eurocheques can also be used for payment in shops, etc. that regularly deal with tourists. See **Crime & Theft**, **Currency**, **Opening Times**.

Trade and Catering Industrial Museum: See **MUSEUMS 1**, **WALK 2**, Kereskedelmi és Vendéglátóipari Múzeum.

Nagy, Imre (1896-1958): A politician who lived in exile in the Soviet Union until 1945 and became Prime Minister of Hungary. In 1956 he led the revolution. He was executed for this in 1958 and buried in an unmarked grave along with thousands of others. In the summer of 1989 they were reburied amid great pomp and ceremony in marked graves.

Nagykörút: The 'Great Boulevard', a 4 km semi-circle linking Margit híd with Petőfi híd, consists of Szent István körút, Teréz körút and Ferenc József körút. Most of the buildings are quite uniform in character but Marx tér is an exception, with the finely-proportioned Nyugati pályaudvar (see **BUILDINGS**) standing opposite the less restrained Skála Metro department store.

National Museum: See Nemzeti Múzeum.

Nemzeti Múzeum: This neoclassical building, set back from the Kiskörút (see **A–Z**) in pleasant gardens, is historically important for its role during the 1848-49 War of Independence (see **WALK 1**). Today, its permanent exhibitions show the history of the nation up to that point. The ground floor has a display of statues and other stone objects dating from the Roman period to medieval times. The first floor is devoted to Hungarian history up to the Magyar conquest of the present territory. Also to be found on this floor are the museum's most popular exhibits, the Hungarian crown jewels. The second floor deals with the later period of the country's history from 896 to 1849. See **MUSEUMS 2, WALK 1**.

Népköztársaság Útja: See Andrássy út.

Néprajzi Múzeum: The Ethnographical Museum is housed in a richly-decorated building on the other side of Kossuth tér from the Houses of Parliament (see BUILDINGS, **Országház**). This museum aims to represent the culture and folk art of Hungarian peasantry as well as the development of early civilization outside Europe. The permanent exhibition on the first floor deals with local works. On the second floor are artefacts from Africa and Asia and more examples of Hungarian art. There are also occasional temporary exhibitions. See MUSEUMS 2.

Newspapers: Most major foreign newspapers are available in big hotels and newsagents the day after publication and cost around 60-250 Ft. *Time* and *Newsweek* are also on sale. There is an English/German language paper published in Hungary called the *Daily News* which costs 8 Ft and appears daily except Tuesdays. It is useful for cinema and theatre listings. See **What's O**n.

Nightlife: Budapest is not a particularly lively city in the evening and nightlife either centres around the theatre, concerts and other cultural performances or a good meal accompanied by a gypsy band. Although there is no one particular concentration of night clubs, most of them are in the Pest area or attached to the big hotels. See NIGHTLIFE.

Opening Times: These vary considerably, but generally:
Food Shops – 0700-1900 Mon.-Fri., 0700-1400 Sat.
Durable Consumer Goods – 1000-1800 Mon.-Wed., Fri.; 1000-2000
Thu.; 0900-1300 Sat.
Museums – 1000-1800 Tue.-Sun.
Post Offices – 0800-1800 Mon.-Fri., 0800-1400 Sat.
Banks – 0900-1700 Mon.-Fri., 0900-1400 Sat.

Operaház: Designed in Italian neo-Renaissance style by Miklós Ybl,
the National Opera House was completed in 1884. Modernization and
restoration to celebrate its centenary has preserved its elaborate interior
and cleaned up the statues of Liszt (see **A-Z**) and Erkel (founder of the
State Opera Company). Tours of the interior allow you to admire the
almost overpowering decoration, the four-tiered gallery and Károly
Lotz's frescoes. See **BUILDINGS, CUTLURE, WALK 3**.

Országház

Országház: In spite of the dome in the middle, it is easy to see that the Budapest Parliament building is modelled on its British counterpart in London. It was designed by Imre Steindl and, at the time of its construction (1885-1902), was one of the biggest buildings in the world. Guided tours show off the richly-decorated interior to the full, Mihály Munkácsy and Károly Lotz being two artists featured. Part of the tour involves an explanation of the way Parliament functions. These tours are likely to become less frequent in view of recent political upheavals and need of the rooms for official purposes. See **BUILDINGS**.

Orientation: Budapest is divided north to south by the Danube (see **Duna**). To the west lies Buda, containing the Castle District (see **WALK 2**) and Gellért Hill (see **PARKS**, **Gellérthegy**). East of the river is Pest, the commercial and administrative centre, the boundary of which is formed by the Nagykörút (see **A–Z**). The area around Erzsébet tér (see

A–Z) more or less forms the centre. Towards the north of Buda and Pest the Danube divides and reunites to form Margaret Island (see **PARKS**, **Margitsziget**). A good street-map is essential for finding your way around, but note that several streets and squares have recently changed their names as a result of the political changes in Hungary. Addresses give the district in Roman numerals, the street name, then the number. *Utca* (u.) – street; *út or útja* – avenue; *tér or tere* – square, *körút* (krt.) – boulevard; *híd* – bridge; *hegy* – hill; *liget* – wood.

Parking: See Driving.

Parliament: See Országház.

Passports & Customs:
As well as a valid passport, foreign visitors from some countries should have a visa. Exceptions include citizens of Austria, Cuba, Cyprus, Denmark, Finland, France, Italy, Malta, Norway, Spain, Sweden, Germany and countries of Eastern Europe. Visas can be obtained from the Hungarian Consulate or IBUSZ travel agencies (see **Tourist Information**) and take 24 hr to issue (postal applications are accepted). They are usually valid for six months and allow a stay of thirty days with two entries into the country. You can also obtain a visa on entry to Hungary at the airport, the road crossing point or the Danube River Port but not if you enter by train. To apply for an extension contact the Foreigners' Registration Police in Rudas László utca 48 hr before expiry. There is no restriction on the amount of money you can bring into Hungary. On leaving, you may change a maximum of $100 worth of Forints back into your own currency so long as it does not exceed 50% of the amount you originally changed. For this you will need to show the original exchange form. You are not allowed to take any Forint notes out of the country. See **Money**.

Petőfi Irodalmi Múzeum: A commemorative exhibition of the Hungarian poet Sándor Petőfi (1823-49) and other leading poets such as Radnóti, Móricz, and Déry. It is located at Károly Mihály u. 16 and is open 1000-1400 Tue.-Fri., 1400-1800 Sat., Sun.

Petrol: See **Driving**.

Pets: To bring your pet into Hungary you will need to show proof of a rabies vaccination not more than a year old and a certificate of health from the vet. All dogs on public transport must wear a muzzle and either be muzzled or on a leash in parks. Check that your hotel will accept animals and note that dogs are not allowed in restaurants. See **Rabies**.

Police: Police in Hungary wear blue and grey uniforms. The traffic police wear white caps. In general, the police are friendly and helpful with tourists. See **Crime & Theft**, **Emergency Numbers**.

Post Offices: Post offices deal with telephones (see **A-Z**), telegrams and telexes as well as mail. Normal opening hours are from 0800-1800 Mon.-Fri., 0800-1400 Sat. The central post office is at Petőfi Sándor u. 17-19. Two are open on Sundays and offer a 24-hr service: Szent István krt. 105 (near Western Railway Station); Baross tér 11/c (near Eastern Railway Station). It costs 12 Ft to send a postcard to a non-socialist country and 24 Ft for a letter up to 20g. Within Hungary, other socialist countries and Austria the rates are 4 Ft and 8 Ft. Stamps can also be bought at tobacconists and at kiosks selling postcards.

Premontrei templom: Situated on Margaret Island (see **PARKS**, **Margitsziget**) this chapel was part of a medieval Premonstratensian monastery. During the Turkish occupation, the 12thC Romanesque church was destroyed and it was reconstructed only between 1930-31, using the south wall of the nave. This wall is the only remnant of the original building. In the tower of the chapel hangs the oldest bell in Hungary, dating from the 15thC. It was recently recovered from the ground where it must have lain buried for centuries. See **CHURCHES**.

Public Holidays: 1 Jan. (New Year's Day); 15 Mar. (National Holiday); Easter Monday; 1 May (May Day); 20 Aug. (St. Stephen's Day); 25 Dec. (Christmas); 26 Dec. (Boxing Day).

Public Toilets: There is no shortage of public toilets in parks, stations, museums, etc. They are bright green and take 2 x 2 Ft coins.

Rabies: Rabies exists in Hungary as it does all over continental Europe. Consequently, all animal bites should be seen to by a doctor as soon as possible. See **Health**, **Pets**.

Radio & TV: There are two main Hungarian TV channels with a third on Wednesday and Sunday but nothing is broadcast in English. 95% of the foreign films are dubbed. Many hotels have cable television facilities. Radio stations are currently in the process of being changed.

Railways: Hungarian Railways, or MÁV, boasts an extensive and well-developed network throughout Hungary and offers direct links to major European destinations. Being part of the central-European railways system, reservations can be made from other countries and the usual discount tickets are valid (e.g. Inter-rail, Eurorail). Other reductions are offered for groups of more than six- seven- or ten-day Lake Balaton trips (see **EXCURSION 2**), seven- or ten-day tourist cards and senior citizens (women over 55, men over 60). It is advisable to book

tickets well in advance. For more information on reductions for jour-
neys throughout Hungary contact MÁVTOURS, Andrássy út 35, tel:
1228049. For general train information, tel: 1227860. There are three
main MÁV stations in Budapest: Eastern Railway Station (Keleti): Baross
tér 10, tel: 1224052 (Vienna, Romania, Soviet Union); Southern
Railway Station (Déli): Krisztina krt. 37, tel: 1351512 (Lake Balaton,
Italy, Vienna and Yugoslavia); Western Railway Station (Nyugati): Teréz
krt. 111, tel: 1315346 (Prague, East Berlin).
The local railway network (HÉV) consists of three lines serving villages
and towns in the vicinity of Budapest: Batthyány tér and Szentendre;
Örs vezér tere and Gödöllő; Vágóhíd and Ráckeve. The same yellow
tickets as used for the trams are valid on this network but within the
city limits only. See **Transport**.

Református templom: This neo-Gothic church was designed by
Samu Petz and constructed from 1892 to 1896. The architect left the
raw materials of the church unmasked. The brick walls are in the shape
of a five-cornered star, the symbol of the Reformed Church.
Over the central part of the church is a dome with ten cor-
ners. The colourful stained-glass windows have only recently been restored after being damaged during World War II.
See CHURCHES.

Religious Services: Hungary is predominantly a
Roman Catholic country and Mass can be heard in
Hungarian in most churches.
Parish Church of Erzsébetváros – VII, Rózsák tere 8. Mass in
English or Italian on request.
Synagogue – V, Dohány u. 2-8. 1000 Sat. See CHURCHES,
Zsinagóga.
Scottish Mission – VI, Vörösmarty u. 51. 1000 Sun.

Roosevelt tér: A large square at the Pest end of the
Széchenyi lánchíd (Chain Bridge). It is bordered by the HQ
of the Hungarian Academy of Sciences to the north; the so-
called Gresham Palace is the most attractive building on the

east side; and the Forum and Atrium Hyatt hotels are situated on the south side. Statues of István Széchenyi (József Engel, 1872) and Ferenc Deák (Adolf Huszár, 1877) are in the small park in the centre of the square. See **WALK 1**.

Royal Palace: See Királyi palota.

Saint Stephen's Basilica:
See **Szent István bazilika**.

Semmelweis Orvostörténeti Múzeum:
This museum is situated on the top floor of the birthplace of Ignác Semmelweis (1818-65). He was a doctor whose concern with cleanliness and hygiene in hospitals lead to greater likelihood of the survival of mothers after giving birth. The display illustrates the development of medical treatment throughout the ages.
See **MUSEUMS 1**.

Sightseeing: Most sightseeing tours are operated by IBUSZ, Budapest Tourist and many other tourist agencies. IBUSZ: city sightseeing tours leave from Erzsébet tér and last three hours. Tickets can be bought on boarding or at any IBUSZ office. They include a drink and a stop at the Hilton Hotel (see **BUILDINGS**). Trips start at 1000, 1100, 1400 and 1500 and are conducted in English, French, German and Italian. Budapest by Night tours include a bus tour of the city ending up at the Maxim or Moulin Rouge nightclubs (see **NIGHTLIFE**) where there is a show and meal provided. Tours start at 1930 and end at 0100, late May-31 Oct.
Boat sightseeing trips operate in the summer, beginning at 1000 and lasting three hours. The cost of a ticket includes a coffee and a brief stop on Margaret Island (see **PARKS**, **Margitsziget**). The boarding point is at Vigadó tér. See **Tourist Information**.

Smoking: Cigarettes can be bought at tobacconists and kiosks very cheaply. Local brands and brands made under licence cost between 50-90 Ft and international cigarettes cost about 180 Ft. Smoking is prohibited on city transport and in other public places, but it is not generally frowned upon and a large number of the population smoke.

Souvenirs: See **Best Buys**.

Sports:
Horse racing – X, Dobi István út 2, tel: 1636895.
Trotting – VIII, Kerepesi út 7, tel: 1342958.
Golf – Near Kisoroszi on Szentendrei-sziget (see **EXCURSION 1**). 0800-2000 April-Oct. Daily membership 690 Ft; individual tuition 500 Ft for a 45-min lesson (available Tue., Fri., Sat., Sun. 1000-1600).
Tennis – Tennis Paradise, Hotel Flamenco: XI, Tas vezér u. 7, tel 665699. 0700-2200. There is a covered court available and rackets for hire.
Skating – Népstadion út. 0900-1315, 1600-2015 Mon.-Fri.; 1000-1425, 1600-2015 Sat., Sun. 40 Ft per person.
Horse-riding – Pegazus Tours: Károlyi Mihály u. 5. They will provide information and make bookings.
Swimming – Béla Komjádi pool: II, Árpád Fejedelem útja 8, tel: 1150639. 0600-1700.

State Opera House: See BUILDINGS, WALK 3, **Operaház**.

Stephen, Saint: See István, Szent.

Students: The main office of the Express Travel Agency for Young People and Students is at V, Szabadság tér 16, tel: 1317777. In the Eastern (Keleti) Railway Station there is a 24-hr office. They deal with cheap student accommodation, including Youth Hostels (see **A-Z**).

Synagogue: See CHURCHES, Zsinagóga.

Szabadság Szobor: Erected in 1947 to commemorate the liberation of the country by the Soviet Army. The main figure is a woman
holding a palm branch (to signify peace) and in front is a statue of a
Soviet soldier. The two figures to the left and right symbolize destruction and devastation on the one hand and peaceful reconstruction and
progress on the other. See CITY SIGHTS 1.

Szabadság tér: A large barracks dominated this area until 1898
when it was demolished. The building became notorious following the
1848-49 War of Independence when many men who took part were
imprisoned and then executed there – including Count Lajos Batthyány.
The HQ of Hungarian Television (MTV) is in the rather eclectic building
on the west side of the square – this used to house the Hungarian Stock
Exchange. Opposite this building are the American Embassy and the
Hungarian National Bank. It is not difficult to spot which of the two
memorials in the square is for Soviet soldiers and which commemorates the Hungarians executed following 1848-49.

Szeged: 180 km southeast of Budapest. Pop: 170,000. Motorway 5,
then Road 75; train from Keleti pályaudvar. Szeged is the important cultural, university and economic centre of the Great Plain. It was practically destroyed by a flood in 1879 which necessitated reconstruction.
The most important building is the two-towered Votive Church though
you should try to visit the Serbian Church nearby for its collection of
icons. There is an important Theatre Festival in the summer with open-
air plays performed in the Cathedral Square. See EXCURSION 4.

Szent Anna-templom: This baroque-style church was built
between 1740 and 1762 by Cristoph and Michael Hamon, and Máté
Nepauer. The church has two towers topped by ornate spires and there
are statues of the Virgin Mary and St. Anne above the entrance. Inside
there is an elongated octagonal nave covered by an oval-shaped dome.
The pillared high altar with its statues is by Károly Bebő.
See CHURCHES.

Szentendre: 19 km north of Budapest. Pop: 16,000. Road 11; bus from Erzsébet tér; train from Nyugati pályaudvar; passenger boat from Vigadó tér. An attractive town favoured by artists. The Serbian influence on this town is seen in the churches and merchants' houses which contribute to its unusual atmosphere. The Serbian Ecclesiastical Art Museum has a collection of 18thC art and some superb 16thC icons. The main square, Fő tér, has a cross at the centre which commemorates the town's escape from the 1763 plague. Buildings of interest include the 18thC baroque-style orthodox church known as the Greek Church and an old school-house now housing the Ferenczy Múzeum, named after the Hungarian impressionist painter. A more popular museum is the Margit Kovács museum which houses a comprehensive selection of sculptures by this well-known Hungarian artist. See **EXCURSION 1.**

Szentháromság tér: This, the former centre of Buda's commercial and cultural life, remains the central square of the Castle District (see **WALK 2**). It contains the statue of the Holy Trinity, although this and the other statues are somewhat overshadowed by the Matthias Church (see **CHURCHES**, **Mátyás-templom**), the Hotel Hilton (see **BUILDINGS**) and the former City Hall.

Szent István bazilika: Work began on the building in 1851 following plans drawn up by József Hild to be continued by Miklós Ybl. It was only after the latter's death in 1905 that József Kauser took over and that the church was finally dedicated. A neo-Renaissance design with two towers at the front, the interior is rather gloomy in spite of its size (it is the largest church in the capital). The huge dome is decorated with mosaics by the prolific Károly Lotz. See **CHURCHES**, **WALK 1**.

Szépművészeti Múzeum: The larger of the two art museums in Hősök tere, this imposing building houses a rich and varied collection with numerous permanent exhibitions. Noteworthy examples are its Greek and Roman sections, and old masters – with special attention paid to Italian, Dutch and Spanish painters. Works by Constable, Hogarth and Reynolds are also displayed in the museum. There is a large collection of modern paintings and sculptures with France being particularly well-represented though artists from other European countries are also present. An enjoyable graphic art collection with a selection of prints and drawings lies tucked away in a corner; and there is, naturally, a Hungarian collection too. See **MUSEUMS 2**.

Táncsics, Mihály (1799-1884): An important 19thC poet. He was imprisoned for producing political pamphlets, and freed on 15 March 1848, the beginning of the War of Independence. He was forced to flee after the failure of the 1848-49 revolution and was imprisoned again from 1857-67. He died in great poverty.

Taxis: Taxis are plentiful in Budapest – the pick-up charge is 10 or 12 Ft and then it is 2 or 3 Ft per km. You can either hail them in the street or wait at a taxi stand. The six main taxi companies are: Főtaxi, tel:

1222222; Volántaxi, tel: 1666666; City-taxi, tel: 1228855; Budataxi, tel: 1294040; Rádiótaxi, tel: 1271271; Taxiunió, tel: 1555000. There are also many privately-owned taxis. See **Tipping**, **Transport**.

Telephones & Telegrams: If you want to make international phone calls it is better to go through the hotel switchboard or go to either a post office or the international telecommunications centre on the corner of Petőfi Sándor u. and Martinelli tér (0700-2000 Mon.-Fri., 0700-1900 Sat., 0700-1200 Sun.) In order to book an international call dial 00 and wait for the long distance tone before dialling the rest of the phone number. You can also make international calls from the red public phone booths which take 2, 10 and 20 Ft coins and have clear pictogram-type instructions for use. Local calls can be made from the yellow and green phone booths and cost 2 ft. To book an internal long-distance call dial 01 or 06 if you want to dial directly. Calls are cheaper from 1800-0700. For help with general problems tel: 1172200. Domestic long-distance call information is on 173333 and International long-distance call information on 1186977.

Telegrams can be sent via telephone by dialling 02 but not from public phone booths. Alternatively, go to a post office or the telecommunications centre mentioned above. The Hungarian telephone network is in the process of being modernized and telephone numbers are being altered. All Budapest numbers now have seven digits and begin with a '1' or a '2'. See **Emergency Numbers**, **Post Offices**.

Thermal Baths: One of the most distinctive features of life in Budapest is the profusion of public baths which offer the chance to relax, bathe or enjoy a sauna and massage. Many curative properties are claimed for the spring waters. Most baths open from about 0600-1900 and charge between 30-80 Ft admission. Massage, mud baths, and so on, are extra. Amongst the best establishments are the Gellért Gyógyfürdő in the Gellért Hotel, Kelenhegyi u. 4; the Király Gyógyfürdő, Fő u. 82-86; and the Széchenyifürdő, Állatkerti u. 11.

Tihany: 136 km west of Budapest. Motorway 7 to Balatonaliga, then Road 71; M 7 to Szántód, then ferry. The village of Tihany is situated on

a peninsula of the same name which is a national park renowned for its natural beauty and rich flora and fauna. The main attraction of the village is the abbey church (Apátsági templom). It was built in the 18thC but the crypt which forms the foundations dates from 1055. The charter of the foundation of the abbey dates from 1085 and is the first known text to have been written in the Hungarian language. The adjoining abbey now houses a museum providing a comprehensive introduction to the lake and surrounding region. Interesting examples of vernacular architecture in the village include the houses in Petőfi utca and Csokonai utca with their thatched roofs and walls made out of the local grey stone. See **EXCURSION 2**.

Time Differences: One hour ahead of GMT. From the end of March to the end of September the clocks in Hungary go forward one hour making it GMT + 2 hours.

Tipping: Tipping is as established in Budapest as anywhere else: taxi: 10-15%; waiter: 10% of bill; cloakroom attendant: 3-5 Ft; hotel porter: 20-25 Ft; pump attendant: 5-20 Ft; gypsy musicians: 50-500 Ft.

Tourist Information: Tourist information is primarily the concern of Tourinform who are at Sütő u. 2. Its friendly staff speak several languages and will give you information on all aspects of tourism in Hungary. Information can also be had by phoning 1179800. They are open every day from 0800-2000. There are many travel agencies who handle the more commercial aspects of tourism including IBUSZ, the Hungarian Travel Bureau. They take care of reservations for hotels, theatres and concert halls as well as organizing excursions around the city and throughout Hungary. There are numerous branches of IBUSZ in Budapest and at stations and the airport. Other places offering excursions and sources of information are; Express, Cooptourist, Budapest Tourist, Volántourist and MALÉV Airtours. They also provide guides and interpreters. See **EXCURSIONS**.

Trams & Trolleybuses: These make an ideal way of seeing the city. Trams are yellow with three or four separate sections and offer a

comprehensive network. Normal service operates from 0500-2300 but there are also night services offered by trams 6, 14, 28, 31, 49 and 50. The main routes are indicated on the free city map (see **Buses**). You will need a yellow 8 Ft ticket before boarding either a tram or a trolleybus (these tickets can also be used for the underground) which you should punch into the machine to validate. Alternatively, you can buy a 24-hr ticket for 60 Ft, valid on trams, trolleybuses and the underground but not on buses. See **Transport**.

Transport: Budapest's public transport system is relatively cheap and fairly easy to use once you get used to it. There are four basic ways of getting around the city – bus, tram, trolleybus and underground. There are three public transport information centres:

Southern Railway Station (Déli pályaudvar), tel: 1153287.

Suburban Railway Terminus (HÉV) at Batthyány tér, tel: 1370716.

Szabó Ervin tér 2, tel: 1183583.

You can buy public transport maps here for 20 Ft which have explanations in English and indicate all the transport routes. Unfortunately, the staff, though friendly, do not speak English. Similarly, you can phone FŐVINFORM (tel: 1171173 or 1178288), for information on public transport and traffic but a knowledge of German is helpful. Tickets can be bought from stations, train and bus terminals, tobacconists, travel offices and automatic machines and must be bought in advance for trams, trolleybuses and buses. On boarding, the tickets should be validated by punching them in ticketing machines. Each ticket is valid for one hour on one journey only. Any transfer requires a new ticket. Children under six travel free when accompanied by an adult. Other means of transport include the funicular railway up to the Castle District (15 Ft), the cog-wheel train (between Városmajor and Széchenyi-hegy), the Pioneer Railway (between Hűvösvölgy and Széchenyi-hegy) and the chair-lift (Zugliget and Jánoshegy). See **Buses**, **Trams & Trolleybuses**, **Underground**.

Traveller's Cheques: See **Money**.

Underground: The underground operates from 0430-2310 and comprises three lines: line 1: Mexikói út – Vörösmarty tér; line 2: Örs vezér tér – Déli pályaudvar (Southern Railway Station); line 3: Kőbánya-Kispest – Árpád híd. You need an 8 Ft yellow ticket (same as for the trams) each time you change lines. See **Transport**.

University Church: See CHURCHES, Egyetemi templom.

Vác: 34 km north of Budapest. Pop: 34,000. Road 2; bus from Erzsébet tér; train from Nyugati pályaudvar; boat from Vigadó tér. Christianity was well established here by the 11thC though the present cathedral is barely 200 years old. Particularly good examples of baroque style can be seen round Március 15 tér. Note the Town Hall at No. 11 which dates from 1764 – the year that Empress Maria Theresa paid a visit. The triumphal arch in Köztársaság út was constructed specially for this same occasion. See EXCURSION 1.

Vajdahunyad vára: This castle, a replica of the one belonging to the Transylvanian Hunyadi family, was built between 1896 and 1908. The various attached buildings are copies of original constructions situated in different towns all over the country. There is a Romanesque chapel modelled on the 13thC Benedictine abbey in Ják (Western Hungary). Opposite is a copy of the castle-tower of Segesvár in Transylvania. In the palace courtyard stands the statue of a 13thC royal scribe who wrote the first Hungarian chronicles but whose actual name is not known. See BUILDINGS.

A–Z

Városliget: The City Park dates from the beginning of the 19thC and in 1896 the artificial lake (which serves as an ice-rink in the winter) was added. The park contains the Vajdahunyad vára (see **BUILDINGS**, **A-Z**) and nearby is a statue of George Washington erected in 1906 by Hungarians who had moved to the USA. The Közlekedési Múzeum (see **MUSEUMS 2**) is on the corner of Állatkerti körút. Other major attractions include the Zoological and Botanical Gardens, the Amusement Park, and the Municipal Circus (see **CHILDREN**). Across the street lies the triple-domed Széchenyifürdő (see **Thermal Baths**) which was built in 1909-13 and enlarged in 1926. At the beginning of Állatkerti körút is the Gundel (see **RESTAURANTS 1**) which has a garden where you can eat outside in the summer. See **Parks**.

Veszprém: 110 km west of Budapest. Motorway 7 to Székesfehérvár, then Road 8; train from Déli pályaudvar. Situated a few km north of Lake Balaton, this is the most important historical and cultural centre in the region. The Bishop's Palace (Tolbuhin utca) was built between 1765 and 1776 out of stone that was formerly part of the Royal Palace. St. Michael's Cathedral dates from the 10thC though its present-day form is from the beginning of the 20thC. The remains of the original church can be seen in the 11thC cemetery of Kálvária-hegy. See **EXCURSION 2**.

Visegrád: 42 km north of Budapest. Road 11; bus from Erzsébet tér; train from Déli pályaudvar; passenger boat from Vigadó tér. Standing at an ideal vantage point on the Danube, it is not hard to see why this town has always played an important part in the history of Hungary. No trace of the Roman settlement is visible and the ruins on the hillside are a recent reconstruction of the medieval royal palace. This building was initiated by King Béla IV in the 13thC and became the most splendid in Central Europe following King Matthias' reign in the 15thC. It was completely destroyed during the Turkish occupation (1541-42) and excavation started in 1932. One of the most attractive features is the Hercules Fountain, in red marble and constituting a rare example of Renaissance art in Hungary. A little further up the hill are the remains of the citadel. See **EXCURSION 1**.

Vörösmarty tér: A statue of the poet Mihály Vörösmarty (1800-55) stands in the middle of this pedestrianized square and three sides are lined with buildings barely a century old – whilst the river side has an even newer frontage, including the central box office for concerts and a busy record shop (see **SHOPPING 3**). During the warmer months the square is popular with pavement artists at the Váci utca end. At the other end is Gerbeaud's (see **CAFÉS**). See **WALK 1**.

What's On: Tourinform (see **Tourist Information**) publish a number of pamphlets with information on different aspects of life in Hungary and Budapest. They also publish a German/English monthly magazine called *Programme in Ungarn/in Hungary* which has details of restaurants, concerts, exhibitions, etc., and which can be picked up free from their office or in hotels or travel agencies. See **Newspapers**.

Youth Hostels: To stay in one of Budapest's youth hostels you will need an International Youth Hostel Federation card which you can either get at home or at the Express office in Budapest (V, Szabadság tér 16, tel: 1317777). There is no age limit.

Zsidó Múzeum: The Jewish Religious and Historical Museum can be found next to the Synagogue (see **CHURCHES**, **Zsinagóga**). Its collection consists of many documents and religious relics which give a good picture of the extent of the Jewish presence and influence in Hungary throughout the ages as well as the effects of the last war on the Hungarian population. See **MUSEUMS 2**.

Zsinagóga: One of the biggest synagogues in the world (it has 3000 seats), this Byzantine-Moorish style building was the work of the German Ludwig Förster from 1854-59. Liszt (see **A-Z**) and Saint-Säens have played here. There is a cemetery surrounded by arcades where the victims of fascism – the dead of the Jewish ghetto – rest in mass graves. The Heroes' Chapel is in memory of the heroes who died in World War I. The Synagogue has been badly neglected since World War II and is in need of restoration. The building on the corner is the birthplace of Theodor Herzel (1860). It now houses the National Museum of Jewish Religion and History (see **MUSEUMS 2, Zsidó Múzeum**). See **CHURCHES**.